Secrets, Shame, and Silence

HELEN HAYES

ISBN: 1986545067
ISBN-13:978-1986545068

DEDICATION

This book is dedicated to my mother, Mable Manson, who taught me so much in our short eight years together.

This is also for all the women who may be struggling trying to put one foot in front of the other in this thing called life.

CONTENTS

ACKNOWLEDGMENTS

This book would not have been possible without the knowledge, tears and laughter of Kristen Lang who diligently typed and retyped my manuscript. Kristen's grasp of this material made her far more than a typist, she is my friend.

Thank you to Sally and Jeff Snipes who helped me in so many ways, to not stop until I crossed the finish line, while Jeff kept raising the bar. Thank you to the friends who have encouraged me for so many years.

.

1
MEMORIES OF MOMMA

We thought it was the sound of a large whip snapping. A faint "crack" like a distant firecracker. It sounded like the lion tamer in the circus with his whip, who knew how to make that sound. We later learned that it came from a small hand gun which Daddy used to shoot Momma six times and then shoot himself once. This happened in the kitchen while all of us kids were in the backyard, as it was my brother Stan's twelfth birthday party. It was 1942 and I was eight years old, the baby of seven.

I was in my fifties when I told Kathy, my therapist, about the murder-suicide of my parents and how I didn't want to talk anymore. I felt drained and wanted to go home.

As I moved for the door, Kathy asked, "Are you crying because you told me about the family secrets?"

I blew my nose and asked, "What do you mean by family secrets? That's the only family secret!" I yelled.

"Helen, we'll discuss this further next week when you come back at the same time. O.K.?"

I mumbled, "Fat chance!" and I raced for my car.

Secrets? Family Secrets? What was Kathy talking about?

I didn't have any secrets except one. I didn't talk about Momma and Daddy because no one ever asked, until I went to my first foster home with my brother and sister, or when I went to school. And now Kathy was asking.

I canceled my therapist appointments for the next month. It was so hard to get out of bed. I loved being in bed where I could cry, smoke and write.

Something didn't feel good in my stomach and I knew I shouldn't have told Kathy about Daddy. Especially about when he drank, he smelled and became mean.

Maybe when I get rid of Kathy, I will stay in bed and cry some more. However, the phone call from her came early in the morning. She had an opening and wanted me there in one half hour.

"I'm not talking about my Dad," I said, and she agreed.

Kathy really wanted me to tell her about Momma. At least what I could remember, and I agreed.

"Kathy, I just have little short memories of her because it was so long ago. When I talk about her they seem to become bigger memories, so I will do my best. I really want to be healthy and if this helps, then it's O.K. with me."

And so, I started to tell Kathy about the bad things that happened during my first eight years. At least what I could remember.

Our house had holes in the roof for the rain to drop into all the pots on the floor, and I remember millions of white worms squirming in black sludge under the linoleum that was partially nailed on the top of the drain board next to the sink. But there was also the smell of hot, buttery, baked bread made on the big black wood stove that would drag you by the neck back into the house. The fragrance filled the neighborhood. We never had much food, but I ate a lot of that bread with sugar sprinkled on it.

When I was five years old Momma and I stood looking over the cardboard she and I taped to cover the hole in the front room window which Daddy had broken, to see if he would come staggering down the alley. He staggered often after he had lots to drink. Many times, he hurt Momma and she'd yell for me to go find my brother Don who was finishing high school. He was always playing hockey and constantly fought with Daddy, so Don was never home. I would call his name and wander down the dark street looking for him. Always being cold and scared was just the way it was. I never found Don. He later joined the Air Force when he was seventeen to get away from home.

My brother Larry had a job and was out of high school, he didn't want to see my dad either. He joined the Marines leaving me to continue calling for Don in the dark. I also had a sister Jeanne. I never knew her real name because she left with her two small children when I was six. It wasn't until Momma's funeral that I saw her again.

I once whispered to Momma, "Why don't you get a divorce?"

"Where did you learn that word?" She asked.

How come she didn't answer the question? I always asked questions. I asked mom and my teachers, "Do I go to school tomorrow?" and "Are we gonna' eat supper tonight?" My teacher said I might be a lawyer because I asked so many questions.

I wanted to hold a picture of Momma in my mind because she smiled often. I had her olive skin and dark hair and I smiled a lot too. I could really make her laugh when I tried to pick her up in my arms. I was almost as tall as she was, and I was pretty big for seven.

The picture of the sweet peas climbing up the broken fence is very vivid in my mind. Momma showed me how to tie them to the string and water them. She also taught me to appreciate the fragrance. I was four years old then and the baby of seven children. My brother Harold was ten, Stan was eight and my sister Lorraine was fifteen months older. Because of the violence my oldest sister Jeanne moved out and changed her name. My two brothers, Don and Larry, moved out also. I had Momma all to myself most of the day except for certain times in the morning when we stopped whatever we were doing to listen to the little white radio on the shelf over the sink. It was somehow important to Momma. As we listened to the voice, tears or a smile would come over her face. It was like magic. The man on the radio told us about buying soap and I remember him asking, "Can a woman over forty from a small mining town find happiness?" I can also remember all the words to the songs we sang when Momma took us to church. I watched her lips as she sang, "I come to the garden alone, while the dew is still on the roses…" or "On a hill far away stood an old rugged cross…" Sometimes she would just smile. I thought her smile, the gospel hymns, and just being with her was so special.

In order for us to look beautiful for church, Momma tore pieces of old rags into long strips and rolled our hair every Saturday night, so that we had curls with a pretty bow for Sunday school. The rest of the time I had pigtails. Once, I got mad at Momma for making the same dress for Lorraine and me and I yelled, "Don't dress me like her, we're not twins!" She just gave me that sweet smile again.

When I was seven, my brother Harold stepped from behind a tree to set up fallen bottles for target practice with his friends when a bullet passed through his stomach and killed him. It was an accident. He was fourteen. I watched Momma cry, but Daddy didn't. I don't think I did either. At the funeral, it just seemed as though Harold was asleep.

I couldn't remember many things about Harold, or his funeral, but I do remember things that he taught me. He patiently tried to teach me how to put the "N" back into the alphabet when I forgot it. And he taught me how to tie my shoes. I remember the shoelaces wrapping around his long slender fingers.

On Saturday mornings, Momma let us spend the day in the movies watching Tarzan serials. Chapter One, Two and so on. It was a long walk to the theater, but I didn't mind. When I finally settled into my seat, I could stick two fingers into my mouth and no one would yell at me. Daddy made me wear some funny kind of glove to bed, so that I wouldn't suck my fingers. Sometimes he would put terrible tasting goop on my fingers. I felt free as I scooted down in my seat in the dark theater and watched the excitement.

After I started kindergarten, I don't remember all the things we did all morning, but my real excitement came when I could poke the kid next to me and insist that he or she ask our teacher, Mrs. Hall, if I could sing for the class. I felt a great wave of happiness when she always said yes. I only knew two songs which I learned from the radio. "Don't Sit Under the Apple Tree With Anyone Else But Me." And "Dark Town Strutters Ball." Mrs. Hall only let me sing one song. That was OK because the following day I would poke another kid in the arm. That happiness I felt when I was singing stayed with me all morning. By the time I walked home, the happiness was gone.

Mom was isolated and she didn't have any friends. We had no grandparents, cousins, uncles, aunts and so on. So, when Momma and Daddy died all I had was Lorraine and Stan. The three of us were the only ones who went into foster care. As a freshman in high school Stan went to a boy's reformatory in Washington D.C. for stealing a car with his friend Danny and taking it over the state line. Lorraine just wouldn't bond with me, but I had my music.

I have one picture of Momma and she is very sad. The only things I remember about my Daddy were the times he got mad and hurt Momma. I don't remember his face, only his shiny, high top black shoes. He was of Irish descent from a small town in Missouri. Sometimes he made beer and sauerkraut and the house smelled awful. He often smelled bad and when he did, he got angry. He'd fling his dinner plate filled with food all over the kitchen, and argued with my oldest brothers, Larry and Don, when they got home from high school. He kept a piece of long rubber hose on top of the cabinet in the kitchen and he used it to hit them. As soon as they were old enough, they enlisted in the service to get away from him. They threw that piece of hose about 50 miles away before they left hoping he would leave the rest of us alone. Another of the bad times was when Daddy had our dog, Bob, put to sleep because he barked too much. It was Don's dog and Daddy didn't tell him about it until Don came home from school. Don wanted to kill Daddy with a knife, but Momma got in between them, and they stopped fighting. Don slammed the door as he went out crying for Bob. The dog was healthy, Daddy just did it because he was mean.

I recall tap dancing in my scuffed Buster Brown high top shoes they came from Montgomery Ward where they had been fitted by the X-ray machine that showed where the toes ended. I would dance as fast as I could, jumping and twirling and falling down, hoping that it would make my Daddy happy and he wouldn't get mad. But it didn't work. I mostly remember everyone screaming. I walked around terrified. This was a way of life before I reached nine years old.

2
MY FIRST FOSTER HOME

I don't know how I got there. It could have been a taxi, a car, or a bus. Mrs. Flynn, the nice lady from the welfare department, was next to me. I held my precious cardboard box in my arms. She didn't know what was in it. That was my secret. My flowered bath powder mitt, a gold locket, some crayons, a favorite doll, plus other special things that a nine-year-old might possess. Before Daddy killed her, Momma always read my favorite story to me, "The Little Engine That Could." Naturally, that book was in my box. But the most prized possession in my box was a blue dress with a row of strawberries that went across my chest. I also had Lorraine's hand-me-downs. All of those dresses had been sewn from flour sacks and had little flowers on them and I liked that. The strawberry dress was different from all the others because it came from a store.

We stopped in front of a big, two story, white house which sat on the corner of Perry Street. The lawn rolled down to the sidewalk and a new wooden fence had been built around the side of the yard. My house with Momma had been dark brown with broken windows and lots of weeds coming out of the dirt. The only color I remember came from Momma's sweet peas in the spring and the white snow during the winter, but the snow eventually got dirty also.

The door opened to welcome me. I had no idea that this would be the beginning of a new life. I saw a plump, smiling lady with brown teeth. I smelled her bad breath as she knelt to hug me. She said I could call her Mom or Aunt Delta. I knew she would never be my Mom. Momma always smelled like lilacs and I was scared of this lady. There was no way I would ever let her see what was in my cardboard box. Oh Momma, I thought, I miss you so much. If you don't have a mother to cry to, you just don't cry.

Mrs. Flynn called it a foster home. I realized that this would be my new home if I wanted. Because of our mother's abundant love, I didn't know we had been poor. Once I realized that we had been in a lower scale economically, I knew I didn't want to be like that anymore. What a wonderful feeling to have carpet under my feet. When I saw the piano, I smiled. I wasn't sure what the fireplace was for. Across the top of the wall was a shelf with many small cups and saucers. Mrs. Holden was the name I decided to call her, and she told me that she collected china and that I would be allowed to hold a cup. The small flowers painted on them looked real. The cups felt like paper.

Mrs. Holden had many children in this house. She had two daughters and two sons. Then she had two small boys whose mothers would come and pick them up at the end of the day, plus my brother Stan, my sister Lorraine, and me.

It was the first time I was not the baby and I felt like a big girl. I didn't know where everyone else slept, but Lorraine and I had a room together.

There were many rules to learn in this new house. We had to make our beds every day, brush our teeth twice a day and take our plates to the kitchen after dinner. She asked me again if I wanted to call her Aunt Delta and again I said no and told her that I would call her Mrs. Holden.

In the afternoon, when her boys came home from school, they wanted to play in the yard, but I stayed in my new bedroom and played with the contents of my cardboard box. When Mrs. Holden called me to come to dinner, I hid my cardboard box in the closet. There was so much food on the table, including some things I had never seen before. Everyone moaned when the turnips, parsnips and pears showed up on the table. Even I didn't like them. Everything else was wonderful and different. Everyone was talking and laughing at the same time. It was not like when Daddy was home for dinner. He would get so mad and then he would throw his dinner plate full of food across the room at the wall and we would all rush to clean it up.

I couldn't wait for dinner to finish so I could go back to my possessions again. I sometimes dreamed of going home and sitting with Momma at the table and eating her home-made bread. At least Stan and Lorraine were with me, so I sort of felt safe. And I had my cardboard box. Mrs. Holden's sons, Jim and Tony, and my brother Stan talked about sports, especially football and baseball. I didn't know what football was. Mrs. Holden didn't have a husband, so she talked with all the kids. When she wasn't talking, she was running in and out of the kitchen with more food and desserts. All of the fruits and vegetables came out of her garden. She liked to make fresh apple and cherry pie. Lorraine wanted to learn to cook and clean the house, so she often helped Mrs. Holden. Not me. I was playing the piano and playing outside. The only thing I liked to do in the kitchen was pop the pill in the plastic bag of margarine. I kept kneading it until the color was even and bright yellow and my fingers ached. I never saw Momma do that. We called it butter. When could I wear my strawberry dress again?

When I was twelve, Mrs. Holden told us that we were going to move to a bigger house, and that same scary feeling rolled around in my stomach like a hot ball of fire. I liked our house. We had been there almost four years.

"But where are we going?" I asked.

"Not very far," she replied. "Right down the street to that big house on the corner."

It had a wrap-around porch and I walked by it on the way to school. I slumped with relief, because it was close to the vacant lot the firemen flooded in the winter where I could ice skate after school. It was closer to my friend Nancy's house, but farther away from David's, who played second base with me. Nancy was my best friend. She taught me about horses. In the winter we would ice skate after school and we did our homework together. Her father was from Holland and sometimes I went to Sunday school with them. Her church was the Salvation Army, which was different than the one I went to with Momma, but they also talked about God. Once they let me play the big bass drum simply because I had good rhythm. I really loved that loud sound.

On hot summer days, I would mow the neighborhood lawns to make extra money. The smell of the cut grass was as heavenly as Momma's fresh bread. Nancy and I would spread out a blanket on the lawns, talk about horses and listen to our favorite radio station waiting for the disc jockey to play songs which we had requested by mail. We would dedicate songs to ourselves and everyone in school and at home. Sometimes we would name a special boy and then giggle when we heard it. The two of us dreamed of growing up and owning a ranch with lots of horses. We learned the lyrics to all the songs, loved to smell the grass and we got the best tans. What a summer!

Lorraine didn't like to play outside much. She would get headaches at night and tell me how much she wanted to move. She convinced me to run away from Mrs. Holden's house with her and move in with our older sister, Jeanne. She just lived a few blocks away in a tiny apartment with her two small children. In fact, she and Mrs. Holden sometimes had drinks together. I didn't know Jeanne very well; she liked to drink like daddy. And she smelled like him most of the time. Lorraine believed that Mrs. Holden was very strict. I didn't mind that she asked us to wash our hands before we took all the pictures and knickknacks off the shelves, piano, mantel and tables. We would dust and polish all the wood, and then wash our hands again and put everything back. Lorraine was always looking for a reason to run away. I didn't think Mrs. Holden was too strict. It was better than daddy getting loud and mean. And everything was clean and pretty. Besides, I got piano lessons and I didn't want to leave.

Lorraine said it would be OK, so we ran away together. Why didn't she run away by herself? How often I cried when I was little.

Wanting to play with her, I would run after her yelling, "Rainy, wait for me!"

And she just yelled back, "Go home!"

Now she wanted me to move with her! How could I not? Maybe it would stop her awful headaches. I tried to get rid of them by singing all the songs I learned from the radio. Some Cole Porter and George Gershwin songs that I would sing softly. I guess it made her head stop hurting, because we both fell asleep. I wondered if she missed Momma as much as I did. I never asked her, and we never talked about it.

I only lasted with my sister Jeanne about one week. She

was never there and there was no food. And it was really dirty. When I went back to Mrs. Holden's, she gave me the sun porch by myself and I loved it. When the flowering plum blossomed outside the window, it was just beautiful and peaceful. She let me paint and she helped me hang wall paper with tiny roses. Because Lorraine and I never bonded, I was so happy that she was not around.

Back in my special room, I hid my little white radio under the blankets, so I could listen to the baseball game. My flashlight was helpful as I drew every hit on my paper. In the morning, that paper looked like chicken scratches, but I knew all about baseball and I was going to grow up and marry Duke Snyder.

3
FRIENDSHIP HAS NO EYES

A ten-year-old doesn't take the bus alone very often. I guess that's why I got lost getting to my first job. My neighborhood wasn't very big. Three blocks to school, a bike ride to my piano lessons, and down the alley to my best friend's house. That day I had the slip of paper with the directions in my hand, but I was too excited to look for the landmarks as the bus rolled on into town. My heart started to pound and to keep from really being afraid, I knew I could always ask a grown-up for help. The bus driver was very polite and assured me that I was only off course by two blocks. Spokane wasn't a large city, so I could see the name on the top of the gray six story building. It was the biggest hotel in town but getting there wasn't very pleasant. My appointment was for 10:00 A.M. If Mrs. Sampson, my teacher, hadn't asked me to do it I probably wouldn't have gone. I didn't have much time for being nervous, and I didn't like being late. More than anything, I was happy just to get out of my regular Saturday chores. This was my first job!

I hurried down the shady side of the street because that was the shortest route. Out of the corner of my eye, I saw an old man lying in the doorway. I went faster and got short of breath. My stomach did flip flops and my heart hurt. When I went shopping once a year for new school clothes, there were never any old men lying in doorways. Just smiling, plaster mannequins in colorful windows. The large neon sign seemed to get closer. Hotel Dumont. It was almost 10:15 AM. I tried not to be nervous, but I was. This was not only my first job, but my first trip to a hotel. I took the elevator to room 541. I knocked on the door.

"Who is it?" asked a woman with a velvety, high-pitched voice.

"It's Helen, Mrs. Janis. I'm supposed to be here at 10:00, but I'm late."

"Just a minute, Helen, I'll be right there."

I tried to imagine what she would be like. She had two lady's names. Mrs. and Janis. That pleased me. One of my friends was named Janice, and all grownup ladies were Mrs. I really liked that. Mrs. Janis.

I first noticed the good smell of sweet perfume, like spring flowers. Her grey hair was neatly done, but her eyes were almost closed. I knew she was blind. Mrs. Sampson told me that. My job was to read to her, take her for walks, and maybe become her friend. I knew that friendship had no eyes. Her voice softened, and it made me feel OK to be there.

"Please come in, Helen."

Mrs. Janis pointed to the sofa as she carefully sat down on the rocker. I noticed the freckles on the back of her hands and her soft, pink, shiny nails. I wished mine looked like hers, but when I was confused or scared about anything, I would pick and chew them until they sometimes bled. Her smile was gentle, and her gaze wasn't quite on target.

"Is this your first job, Helen?" she asked.

"Well, I mow lawns for our neighbors and in the winter, I help them shovel the snow," I said proudly. "But you are the only one who ever offered me money. One dollar an hour. Isn't that right?" She smiled again, nodding. Two dollars was a lot of money. I was bursting with excitement, wondering how much candy and gum it would buy. "Do you do a lot of reading along with your school work?" she asked.

"Heck no! If there is time before it gets dark, I go outside and play until dinner." She must just like to smile, I thought.

She handed me a book with a marker where I was to begin. I don't remember anything except the dull humming of my voice. My nose and upper lip were damp. I didn't have pockets for Kleenex, so I quickly used the sleeve of my sweater. The following Saturday, I arrived on time. We didn't read because Mrs. Janis wanted to be in the fresh air and sunshine. I also felt like walking. It wasn't easy describing things in the windows to her. Typewriters, the theatre bills for the movie house next door, and all the stuff in the drug store, plus the prices. She held my arm tightly and smiled a lot, while she gently tapped her white stick. I began to feel very comfortable with her.

She loved the bag of candy I brought on my third visit. Especially when I explained the right way to eat it. The candy corn was triangular, striped orange, yellow and white. You had to bite off the white top and yellow bottom, then eat the orange center last. Sometimes we would have contests to see who could eat the fastest. She made me laugh.

Next time she wanted to listen to music. I saw lots of records in the cabinet by the sofa and quickly figured out how to put them on the phonograph.

I yelled when I heard the clarinet from the orchestra play. "What is that?" I asked. "Who is playing that?"
I didn't want her to answer right away because I wanted

to keep listening, but I was really hungry to know.

"The name of the song is Rhapsody in Blue and George Gershwin wrote it. Do you like it, Helen?"

"Oh, yes," I answered. "I live with a lady who has a big daughter and she plays this for me on the piano. The beginning of the song reminds me of climbing stairs...a long flight of stairs."

Again, she smiled as we sat and listened to some wonderful piano with lots of orchestra. I gazed around the room trying to concentrate. She told me many things about the composer. I learned that George had a brother, Ira, who wrote lyrics. I couldn't wait to tell my piano teacher about all the new things I was learning, and especially to show her the record, Rhapsody in Blue, that Mrs. Janis gave me as a present when I left that day. It was very special to me. I thought about my cardboard box.

Three months had passed when the rains came. I learned to read slower and my nose and upper lip didn't get wet anymore, but my best times were when we would quietly listen to the music. I liked the idea of living in a hotel. It was peaceful and there weren't any chores.

The winter months made my visits to Mrs. Janis's more difficult. The cars and buses were sliding around in the snow, people blasted their horns and people rushed everywhere. After my first trip, I didn't need the directions. I even knew short cuts. December was freezing. One day, like my first day, I was fifteen minutes late. As I walked into the lobby, heading for the elevator as I always did, the manager slowly approached me. He guided me to his office and closed the door. Something terrible had happened to Mrs. Janis. Thursday evening, she had called her doctor because she wasn't feeling well. The ambulance had come and taken her to the hospital where she died of pneumonia on Friday. The manager told me how sorry he was. Tears filled my eyes. I felt like I wanted to vomit. Wait until you're outside, I kept telling myself. I could taste the blood from the inside of my lip where I had chewed it. I thanked him and walked towards the bus stop, feeling the cold tears run down my cheeks. I didn't care who saw me as I wiped my nose on my coat sleeve. She was my best grownup friend, besides Mrs. Flynn, my social worker. There would be no more job, no more reading, walking, music sessions or giggling over the candy. She was gone. Just like Mama.

That afternoon when I got home, I sat on my bed and thought about my special times with Mrs. Janis and I cried. Lots of pictures raced around in my mind. The pretty blue sofa and the fringe on the lamp. I thought of her when I listened to familiar melodies on my little white radio. Maybe someday, I would have my own record player so that I could play "Rhapsody in Blue."

4
LAZY DAYS OF SUMMER

Now that school was out, I started to feel more comfortable. Our street was quiet, and I played baseball with my new friends from the neighborhood; Nancy, Joanie, and David. We used the fence around our house as first base and the telephone pole across the street as third base. For our second base and home plate, we could use a rock or draw with chalk. If a car came, we'd stand on the curb. I watched Stan and learned a lot without asking any questions. The boys thought I knew the rules. But one time, I hit the ball really far. I went around first and second. Gasping for breath, I touched third base but kept running to slow myself down. Stan caught the ball on third, and as I came back slowly to touch the base, he tagged me, and I was out. I screamed that you could run past first and be safe and they screamed, "Not on third!" How was I supposed to know? No one ever told me, and I hadn't asked. I was furious, because they laughed at me.

On March 29, I had my first birthday party, eight months after Mama died. I was nine years old. I remember all the kids sitting around the decorated table. Two boys I'd played baseball with, two girls from school, Stan and Lorraine and all the other foster kids. I remember feeling warm and special as I opened each gift. Everyone was watching me, and I felt that good feeling like I did when I sang for my class. I liked it, especially when they all sang Happy Birthday. Everything was so different now. No fighting and screaming, just my secret aching for Mama. Mrs. Holden's oldest daughter Rosie played the piano beautifully. She was about seventeen years old and she taught me the names of composers such as Cole Porter, George Gershwin, Vincent Youmans. She said I could practice her music which she kept neatly under the lid of the brown piano bench. It was too hard to play because the music had lots of sharps and flats and I was only learning Book Two of John Thompson, but I learned every word of the songs and could play the melodies with one finger.

There's a somebody I'm longing to see. I hope that she turns out to be, someone to watch over me.

I changed the word he to she and thought of Mama watching over me when I sang it. I knew she was because Lorraine told me so. Rosie also had records of the Andrews sisters, Tommy Dorsey, Art Tatum and Harry James. If I was careful, she said I could play them when my friend Nancy came over after school.

When I finished Book Two of my piano lessons, I was ready for my first piano recital at school. Maybe I could wear my strawberry dress. I was ten years old and this was a special occasion. I raced home from school and upstairs to my room and pulled my cardboard box from the closet. There it was, that beautiful blue dress that matched the sky on a cool summer day. The small red strawberries on the front that looked so real with their long stems connected, the lace around the collar and the ribbons that tied into a bow in the back. I held up the dress to my body. It looked like it would fit a doll. How could this be? I had been saving it for a special day. My heart felt like it stopped, and tears spilled out over my lashes and down my cheeks. I sat on the floor of the closet for a long time just looking at the awful smelling bath powder mitt, the tarnished gold locket and my book, "The Little Engine That Could." I had never told anyone about the secret feelings for Mama and her death, and how sad I felt. There was only one person who would ever understand. Oh Mama, please come and hold me. I feel so little, but I am ten years old now.

Mrs. Holden took me down to the wallpaper store to pick my wallpaper for one wall in my room. Lorraine was more interested in learning how to cook than decorating. I'm happy she had her own room. She gave me a bucket, a sponge and some water. Her daughter, Suzie and I put up the wallpaper by ourselves and it was perfect. Then we painted the three walls in a light blue that matched the little bouquets of blue flowers floating through pink ribbons. I hung pictures of Peggy Lee, Jo Stafford, Duke Ellington and Frank Sinatra under the window near my bed. My bedspread was pink to match the ribbons and there were white, frilly pillows propped up against the headboard.

I listened to music when I did my homework and looked out my window and saw the flowers on the plum tree. Daydreaming made me feel powerful. I dreamed of horses, piano recitals and Mama. There was a war going on, so Mrs. Holden would give me one dime before I went to school every Monday morning. During the winter, I would put the dime in the finger of my woolly glove or tie it in the corner of my hankie to keep it safe. Sometimes I lost it in the snow. When I got to school, I would give it to my teacher, Mrs. McElroy, and she would give me stamps for my savings book that I was supposed to exchange for War Bonds. I bought my first bicycle when I had saved enough to fill two books, instead of buying a War Bond. With the next book, I bought ice skates. This was a very happy time for me, filled with peace. Stan left me his collie, Shep, when he went to the boy's reformatory. Shep looked just like Lassie. Shep always came with Nancy and me on our lazy summer days of dreaming.

Summer had ended, and snow covered the sidewalks. On Christmas, Mrs. Holden handed me a big decorated box. When I opened it, I saw a beautiful little white radio almost like Mama's. I thought that only grownups got presents like this and maybe it meant that I was becoming a big girl. In three more months, I would be thirteen and now I had my own radio.

I remember one incident where I discovered that I had a terrible temper. Mrs. Holden's son, Jack, came into the kitchen. I was there with Shep. He didn't like the dog in the kitchen, so he threw Shep down the stairs into the basement. When I heard Shep howling and the thumps as he rolled down the stairs, something inside me turned into that same hot ball of fire I felt when Daddy was hurting Mama and when I first heard we were going to move. I was standing at the sink and I picked up all the glasses in the dish rack and threw them at Jack. There must have been at least eight or nine. Glasses hit the doors, walls and hit Jack's back. Shattered glass went everywhere. Especially into the big pot of chili which was simmering on the woodstove. I was screaming, crying, and trying to get to Shep as Jack held my arms. Mrs. Holden's daughter Suzie came running downstairs. When she saw the pot of chili with the big pieces of glass sticking out, she reached over and slapped my face. She didn't even stop to ask what happened. Mrs. Holden's other son came in and called me a crybaby. That made me feel awful. I wasn't a crybaby. It was at that point in my life when I decided to cry only when I was happy. When I got a nice present, or I heard a special song or in the movie when Lassie came down the road home. Twice a year I would give myself permission to feel sorry for myself and I could cry. But no more than twice a year. I yelled at

Suzie that I would run away. It was a long walk back to my sister Jeanne's place. I stayed until she came home, and she took me back to Mrs. Holden's the next day. Nothing was ever said about the chili or Jack hurting my dog, Shep, and things settled down again.

As in the past, I got many wonderful things and many nice things happened, like getting my white radio, learning the piano, buying new clothes and eating the good food Mrs. Holden cooked. I loved life, and no one ever hurt Shep again. The better things got, the less I thought about Mama.

During this time, I was convinced that I was dying of the disease I had heard about called cancer. When I discovered there was blood all over my panties, I screamed for Lorraine to come to the bathroom. She mumbled something and said that I was all right and that this would happen to me every month. Lorraine reached into the cabinet under the sink and handed me a thick, white gauze pad. I was confused by what was happening to my body. I didn't share this with my girlfriends and Lorraine and I never talked about it again. Just like with Mama when she wouldn't talk to me about most things if I asked her. The bleeding lasted seven days and when it happened next month, I got my own pad from under the cabinet. That's the way it was in our family. Secrets and never talking about what was going on.

I left what I had at Mrs. Holden's for a life of loneliness at Jeanne's. Being with my two sisters was very important to me as they were all the family I had. This was my first experience learning about triangles and they don't work for me. Not much food, sometimes no wood or coal for the stove. I hated it when the kitchen floor was covered with water because one of us hadn't emptied the pan under the ice box. Sister or no sister, I wanted to move back into my room at Mrs. Holden's, so one day after school, I went over to see her, and she said that I could move back into my old room. Lorraine didn't want to go so she moved across town with a lady named Grace. I never knew Grace. Stan was now in Washington DC and we were never a family anymore. I was very lonely.

5
LIFE IS FALLING APART

While my life was improving, Stan's was getting worse. At 15, he started stealing hub caps with his friend, Danny. Then Danny and Stan decided to steal a whole car and take it for a ride. They didn't realize that when they took the car across the state line to Idaho that it became a felony. I loved Stan, but not when he held my head under the water at the public swimming pool where we spent a lot of time during the summer. I'd felt as if my body was going to explode when he finally let my head up. As I gasped for air, he laughed. I screamed at him for laughing at me, but he was serious. I didn't do anything to him, so why would he do that? I think he missed Mama and Daddy. He had always been Daddy's favorite. Stan was sent far away to a boys' reformatory in Washington D.C. I wrote to him often at first because I really missed him, and I loved him. He answered my letters and told me to spend my allowance on the new record by Frankie Laine called, "Lucky Old Sun." When Stan was arrested and taken away, no one ever told me what actually happened, and we never talked about it again, not even in our letters.

I think Stan was angry because when he was two years old, he got polio. Everyone said it was from swimming in the public pool. On the radio a famous lady from Australia named Sister Kenny said that if you kept hot towels around the affected leg every two hours, you could cure it. Mama was so busy that she didn't always have time to do the towels, and Daddy would get real angry because of that and then he would hurt her. Stan thought it was his fault that Daddy hurt Mama. Daddy wanted Stan to be well, because they always did many things together on Saturdays. Neither Lorraine nor I were ever asked to go along. Stan was the only one in the family who didn't have brown hair and eyes like Mama. His hair was so blond that it looked almost white. I wished that I could remember more. The summer when Stan was taken away just flew by. After a few months, I stopped writing to Stan and I never saw him again until I was fifty years old.

I was very popular in school and my friends all wanted to know why I lived at the Holden's house. I told them I lived there because my parents had died.

Again, they said, "Oh, in a car accident?"

I would hesitate and then say, "yes."

That was the beginning of hiding the truth and truly understanding that I had told a lie.

I put on weight from eating all the food and desserts Mrs. Holden made, and the strawberry dress just disappeared from my cardboard box. Mrs. Holden took me to buy new clothes at Montgomery Ward's, Sears and Penny's. We had so much money from being on welfare that I could wear a different outfit every day. I had wool sweaters when it was cold and cotton blouses when it was hot. I had shoes that fit. Mrs. Holden's daughter, Suzie, made me wool pleated skirts and flannel nightgowns we called Tommies. She even made plastic bags to keep my sweaters neat in the drawer. I don't know if Lorraine or Stan also got nice things like me, but I bet they did. Mrs. Holden got welfare money every month for all of us. One day we were very poor and the next day we had lots of money. That really confused me.

Half way through the summer, she decided to marry a man named Marvin. He was there for every Sunday dinner and he always seemed to have a glass of beer in his hand. He played wonderful music on the saxophone and helped me with my piano, but he had that same smell as Daddy. How could I ever forget that?

Things were now changing very fast. I was getting ready to graduate from grammar school on Friday, and I would start high school on Monday. I was terrified, but Lorraine was already there so maybe that would make it easier for me and we could finally bond. Living with this hope only reminded me of when she ignored me as a child and Mama would wipe the tears from my dirty face and give me some bread with sugar sprinkled on top.

Mine was the last class to graduate in January 1949. There were twelve of us who had been together for almost five years and now we were all going to different high schools. I would miss them all. Especially Nancy. She was going to the school that her cousins were already attending. No one understood why I cried so much about that. When I was a freshman, I saw Lorraine in the halls, but she barely spoke to me. She had her own friends and was still living with Grace. I didn't see Lorraine much until she got married at eighteen to John, who sometimes smelled like Daddy, too.

6
LEAVING MY FIRST FOSTER HOME

My first year in high school really scared me. Boys were so tall, girls had big breasts, and there were hundreds of kids in the hall, yelling and laughing. I soon learned about sororities which were supposed to be underground. There must have been five of them and it wasn't long before someone slipped an envelope into my hand in the hallway. I was thrilled because these were invitations to join their group. I felt so special and was really excited. They were names I'd never heard before, such as Tau Sigma and Tri Zeta. I was going to have lots of friends, and this was going to be a wonderful year for a 14-year-old.

Towards the end of my freshman year, I raced home after school with my invitations to show Mrs. Holden and Marvin. She was standing at the sink cutting up peaches, and he was drinking a beer. When I asked permission to join one of these clubs, Mrs. Holden didn't answer. Marvin told me that it was out of the question. He simply said that girls drank beer and smoked cigarettes, and that he wasn't going to let me be any part of it. I had homework and piano to keep me busy. Well, something inside of me burst and that hot ball of fire formed in my stomach again. That same feeling when my dog, Shep, was thrown down the stairs, and when Daddy was hurting Mama.

I screamed, "I didn't ask you. You're not my Dad. I'm going to join one of them, and I don't care what you say."

Before I knew what happened, Marvin reached over and grabbed my arm and threw me over his lap. His large hand hit my butt about six times. I wiggled, screaming and crying. Then suddenly my mind flashed back to Mama. Just because I talked back to Marvin, didn't mean that he could spank me. Mrs. Holden didn't say one word to stop him. I was 14 years old, had started my period, and wore a bra. Nobody was going to hit me ever again.

I ran off screaming, "I hate you. I'm not going to live here anymore. I hate you."

I sat on my bed in my beautiful room with the flowered wallpaper and all my pretty things and cried. After dinner, I cried some more and decided to call my social worker and friend, Mrs. Flynn. She was very surprised to hear from me after our last conversation when I called to tell her about friends, my new bra, getting my period, and how happy I was to be starting high school. She always made me feel very good when we talked, but now I wanted her to get me out of there and away from Marvin fast. Besides, I had flunked Algebra. X+Y=Z meant nothing to me. No one was ever going to hit me again.

My radio went into the cardboard box with all my things and I got into the car, along with my dog Shep, and sat next to Mrs. Flynn. I was so hurt and scared that I didn't turn around as we pulled away from the house that had so many wonderful memories. I would not tell anyone how ashamed I was for being spanked at 14 years old. I never saw the Holdens, Nancy, Joanie or David or anyone from that part of town ever again. Everything was dead as far as I was concerned. I was going to start a new life again on the South Hill in Spokane with Betty and Gene. They were to become my next parents and I would start my sophomore year in a different school. Lorraine and I didn't speak much, and Stan was away. I knew that the South Hill was really the best place to live in town, and I would never look back. Another new start with fresh paint!

7
THE SOUTH HILL,
CIGARETTES AND UMBILICAL CORD

Betty was a school teacher and Gene worked for the railroad. They had adopted a daughter, Anne, at birth. She was now eight years old. I had my cardboard box, my dog, Shep, and my own bedroom. Betty and Gene let me paint it. I chose to paint the walls a beautiful, pale green and the trim plain old white. It was very peaceful, and I loved it. It was like a fresh start and I didn't have to look backwards. Betty painted three walls in her bedroom pink and one wall chocolate brown. Oh my!

My new home had a fireplace, a carpet that went almost to the walls, a new little sister and only two secrets. At 15, I was smoking cigarettes. I learned this from the other kids in Mrs. Holden's neighborhood as we all hung out on warm summer nights. Smoking made me feel so grown up. Betty and Gene didn't have to know. Betty quickly arranged for me to meet a new friend. Kay lived close enough so that we could walk to the school bus stop every morning. I felt so different now. This was the South Hill. Everyone had enough food to eat and nice cars. High school was wonderful. I had never thought about having a boyfriend until I met Kay, who already had Ken. I really wasn't too interested, but I learned a lot from her because she talked about him all the time. He would get his dad's car and they would go out on the bluff and kiss a lot. That seemed kind of silly compared to my many constructive activities. I had a quota of book reports I wanted to turn in by the end of the semester. I truly wanted to please my teacher.

My first day with Betty and Gene was a real eye-opener. Gene said that he was going to the store before dinner and asked me if I needed any cigarettes. I almost fainted. I felt real hot and didn't want to lie to him on my first day there. How in the hell did he ever know that I smoked? I'd blown the smoke out the small window and flushed the evidence. He wasn't even home from work when I did that. God! I really like this guy. He was one smart man! He called my bluff!

After dinner, he offered me a cigarette and he gave me a gold cigarette case and a new lighter. But I found I could not put the cigarette to my lips after I finally got it going. Instead, I only flicked off the ashes. I still didn't want to admit the truth, but I didn't want to lie either. Actually, I had never smoked in front of an adult before. I wanted to throw up!

His only comment was, "If you are going to smoke, you are going to smoke at home. But someday you are going to want to quit!"

"Oh, I can quit anytime I want," was my reply.

His other comment to me that first night was, "Helen, you can have a place to hang your hat or you can have a home. Which do you want?"

I was really scared because no one had ever spoken to me like that. Especially as an individual. I was always addressed as a part of a group around the table or in the classroom. I mumbled something about wanting a home and I remember feeling really good inside, as I smiled at all three of them.

I started to take the dishes to the kitchen the way I learned at Mrs. Holden's house. When Betty cooked, she used every pot and pan in the kitchen, so I knew I would be there for a while. I washed, and Betty dried. All the while she was telling me something about sex. After one hour, the only thing I remember from her talk was "umbilical cord." I was happy I didn't know what she was talking about. I was happy that she corrected me from saying "I don't want no more." And then explaining about double negatives. No one else had ever talked to me like I was a grown up. And I was. I was going to be sixteen and I had just made the biggest decision of my life and that was that I was never going to run away again. Or at least, that's what I thought then.

I loved my sophomore year. Betty and Gene let me join a social club and they let me smoke. I had a lot of friends and I was finally on the "south hill", the best part of town. I read many books, gave lots of book reports, got good grades, loved to wear short shorts, sweat shirts and have bare feet.

My friends always told me how great my legs were, especially when they were tan. I remember at Mrs. Holden's house when I was twelve, one of the older boys said, "If I had legs like yours Helen, I would walk on my hands." As soon as I got home, I told everyone at the dinner table what he said. They all laughed. I started to cry because I didn't understand any of it. I hated it when they all laughed at me.

Near the end of my first term, Gene announced that he had taken a job with the railroad in California. My first thoughts were to move to another foster home so that I could keep getting a welfare check, and how much I would miss Betty and Gene and Anne. But when they asked if I wanted to go with them, all I knew was that I didn't want to move in with another family. I said yes to California and goodbye to all my friends again.

Gene went down ahead of us to get a house. Betty, Anne and I drove down later. I don't know why, but I thought we would be back in a few months, so I willingly left my collie dog, Shep, with the neighbors. We couldn't take him in the car, and I just didn't understand, so I didn't put up a fight for Shep. I never saw him again and it made me very sad and angry. Because of how she lied to me about Shep my feelings towards Betty began to change. I didn't trust her.

Stan was in a boy's reformatory and Lorraine was still with Grace back on the North Hill, and I was going to see the Pacific Ocean for the first time.

My first trip with Betty to San Francisco was to see her friends. My stomach and heart felt as if they would explode with joy. The Golden Gate Bridge was so beautiful and all the tall buildings kind of scared me. The only tall building I had known was the Hotel Dumont when I was ten. Betty took me to the Fairmont Hotel on top of Nob Hill. I was really afraid that our old car would not make it up to the top. What if the cable car brakes didn't hold? We were right behind it. There was the sensation again, that hot ball of fire in my stomach. I didn't say a word to Betty and she finally parked the car. We walked into the hotel and I gasped at the beauty of the red carpet and the enormous lobby. Was I seeing this on a movie screen? All I knew was that I didn't want to leave the hotel. Maybe someday I could figure out how to rent a room there forever, or perhaps work there. I thought that moving to Mrs. Holden's house had been the best thing that had happened to me after Mama died. Then

I moved onto the South Hill for a while and that was wonderful. Now I was standing in the lobby of the Fairmont Hotel and I thought I was in Heaven. How far did this world go and how many more beautiful things were out there for me to see?

The one bad thing I remembered when we got into the San Francisco area was the brown hills. There was so much sun all the time and so little rain that nothing ever got as green as it did in Spokane. But I still loved it. My new school, Hayward Union High School, was the biggest school I had ever been to. It had a 45-acre campus and was a replica of the White House in Washington, D.C. It was my first experience of seeing a black person and he was president of the student body. I thought he had a better tan than I did! My class went to Santa Cruz for a field trip and I got to ride in a car driven by a classmate who had her license and smoked. The other three girls in the car knew each other and they invited me. We all smoked in the car and that felt so grown up. The ocean was just as I imagined from the movies. I thought I was in heaven with the hot sun, sand, my shorts and bare feet. Life was wonderful again!

I didn't know what happened to Gene's job, but it was over, and we were heading to Portland, Oregon. I said goodbye to friends again at school and I promised that I would write. Sadness never entered my mind. I kind of liked this gypsy life and I had another bedroom I could paint.

8
MY FIRST JOB

I found a new friend at the bus stop named Caroline. She had thin lips, curly short blond hair and a very high voice. She lived down the street and the one thing I definitely knew was that her dad smelled like my dad. He loved his beer.

I spent a lot of time at her house after school doing homework. When her dad got home from delivering the mail, he loved quizzing us about baseball, history or movies. He was a very funny man, but some of his teeth were missing when he smiled. That was awful. Caroline and I loved music and she could harmonize to all the songs we sang. Oh, how I wished I could do that! We sang everything we heard on the radio and Caroline knew every song from the plays on the New York stage, the popular radio show The Hit Parade and which song won at the Oscars' each year. I was amazed that she knew this stuff, but then I never asked anyone else if they knew it. Caroline is the only person that I knew who could identify all the John Philip Sousa marches by name. I knew them all, but I had a hard time keeping the names straight. We constantly tested each other by singing them and then guessing the titles. She didn't play an instrument and I had that little bit of piano at Mrs. Holden's house.

I didn't go to the Senior Prom. Graduation went very fast and I felt very lonely. Betty said I couldn't go on to college because they didn't have the money. That meant I had to get a job. How the hell do you do that? I hadn't a clue, but then I never painted a bedroom before either.

Jantzen was the largest manufacturer of swim wear and I loved to swim. The two buildings took up a couple of city blocks, because one building where I had to go was filled with people all dressed up and in offices. Mrs. Roberts called me into her office which had pictures of beautiful ladies in swim suits all over the walls. I felt very comfortable with her and I actually forgot all the lies I had planned on the bus and all of the prayers I had said. I knew I wanted to work with her.

I waited in her office while she answered the buzzer on her phone. Should I say my typing skills were 60 words per minute or the truth of 40 words per minute? I typed close to 30, so I decided to tell her that I typed 50. She smiled at me as she hung up the phone.

"Helen, are you here for the secretarial position?" she asked.

"Yes, I am," I replied.

"I'm so sorry, but the position was filled this morning," she said as my heart sank with relief over my typing skills.

"I would like to look at your legs, Helen."

Oh, God, this is it. I knew they would try to kidnap me and no one would know where I was, and it would be hours before they would know that I was even missing. As I stood in front of her ready to bolt out the door, I gently lifted my skirt while she looked at the legs.

"Would you mind taking this note over to this lady in the other building across the parking lot and tell her that I sent you?"

I said "O.K." and usually I did exactly what I was told.

Maybe I would stop and call home, so someone would know where I am, just in case I ended up in the back of a black car being kidnapped. It was just a quick drive over one of the many bridges and I would be in another state.

Being superstitious was helpful. I knocked on wood a lot. Sometimes I would say, "Oh God! What am I going to do?" I repeated this very phrase all the way to the new building.

If I thought the worst, it turned out to be the best. I didn't understand any of it and I didn't care. I was going for a new job in the big world and I was just 17 years old.

It was a long walk to the huge warehouse building where Mrs. Roberts had sent me. I pulled open the door and saw rows and rows of women sitting at sewing machines, chatting quietly and listening to their radios. They were making swim suits. I found the room number on the paper Mrs. Roberts had handed me and I knocked on the door.

When she opened the door, I thought I was looking at Carmen Miranda, my favorite movie star, without the basket of fruit on her head. Her accent was very thick. She said her name was Mrs. Bandolino and she explained that she designed the swim suits and she wanted me to model them for a big show that was coming soon. I told her that I didn't know how to model, and she explained that she would show me. I left the building, heading for the bus home. I was so excited and felt so powerful because many girls would love to do the job that I was just offered. I didn't even ask if I would get paid. That was the first of many modeling jobs.

I still needed more work and was entered in the Miss Oregon Press Photographers contest. At this point I walked the runway with plenty of experience but was still scared. What the hell was I doing? My boss at Jantzen talked me into it. I was now 18 and anyone could talk me into anything. Three days later I got a call from the head of the Public Relations Department of Pac Bell. During the interview, he told me that I would stand in front of 100 to 500 people explaining about all the latest gadgets coming out of the Bell Labs in New York. I smiled and said yes, but I didn't understand a word he said.

Later I learned I would have an expense account, plus food and lodging and a driver to travel all over the state of Oregon. I felt as though I was taking the first step off a cliff into a great black hole. I guess that's what is called growing up!

9
MY FIRST APARTMENT

I kept the secret of my new employment from Betty and Gene as long as I could. Betty laughed when I suggested getting a job and an apartment.

Her lips puckered, and she said, "You will have a lot of problems finding a job because you aren't very smart, Helen."

I heard myself gasp the deepest breath and after dinner I raced to Caroline's. Ruby was a classmate of ours and had told Caroline earlier that she was looking for a roommate to share the expenses. I called Ruby and took a look at this very small apartment that next evening. As we sat smoking on the dirty green sofa, I felt the greatest sense of freedom. I had a new apartment on the ground level and on the corner. It was so small that we just stuffed our clothes in the dinky closet and personal stuff under the twin beds. Outside the kitchen window I could see the lawn that someone took care of and some flowers someone had planted. There was so much that I needed to learn fast.

"Ruby, I have two jobs now, but I know nothing about living on my own. This has all happened so fast."

"Don't worry about it, Helen. I'll explain how the bills are paid and you can cook what you like," she said.

"But I don't know how to cook, Ruby."

"Well, I'll show you how to keep from burning down the house."

I didn't see Ruby much that summer as I was traveling all over the state for my job. Gene said car insurance was too expensive and I couldn't get a driver's license.

When I told my new boss that I couldn't take the job, he said, "Don't worry, Helen! We'll get you a driver!"

We crisscrossed the state as I explained to groups of 200 to 500 people about the latest things that were coming out of the Bell Labs in faraway New York, and I'm still a teenager.

I didn't learn to cook during that time as I was living in hotels and eating in restaurants, but I did have my first drink. Associating the drinking with my family never stopped me from having fun. I saw Bette Davis, in one of her movies order a martini, so I did also. It made me sick, but it seemed to compliment the filet mignon, creamed spinach and a baked potato. It was the fifties.

"I just met a wonderful guy, Helen," Ruby said. Her face looked down away from my eyes. "He came into my work at the bank and asked me to lunch. And I'm going to stop seeing Gary and spend all my time with Louie because I'm really starting to like him enough to get married."

All I could say was that I was happy for her. I would just find a new roommate and a new place to live. Maybe I could paint my room in a new apartment.

That summer Ruby and Louie decided to get married and I found a new apartment and a new friend, Susan, to share the expenses. Three years had sailed by and Ruby and

I had just had a big party to turn 21. I had my voter's card in one hand and my liquor card in the other, so I could buy, and I was ready for anything.

I did a pretty good job by myself. I would never ask Betty because she said I would always fail because of my childhood, but I was with Jantzen part time for four years and Pac Bell for five years.

It was very shortly afterwards that my new friend and co-worker, Jennie, suggested that we move to San Francisco. All I had was a few clothes, the stuff under the bed, and a box from my first foster home. One of these days I will open it, but not today! I'm heading for San Francisco!

10
ROOMMATES AND ROMANCE

Jennie and I were ready and excited to get out of that old beat-up Chevy that we had been in for 8 hours. I had my cardboard box from my foster homes, a few possessions and my clothes. I had one thousand dollars and the prospect of a job back with Pac Bell.

We stayed in a beautiful hotel while we raced around looking for a great apartment. Jennie had heard of another girl, Maxine, and she agreed to join us in sharing the rent. Max was an excellent cook, loved shoes and clothes, and she and I had some wonderful drinking nights together. Jennie was also an outstanding cook, and I still knew little about the kitchen.

We all finally agreed on an apartment on Broadway, and with my name, identical to the first lady of theater in New York, I was so happy! What conversations I would have! As we were young and, in our twenties, we had a lot of cocktail parties in our beautiful apartment. When we went up on the roof deck, we could see the fabulous Golden Gate Bridge. I loved that place!

One Saturday night we had over 80 people up for a Martini/Manhattan party. I met Ted, who was from the office building next door. I think Max invited Ted. Evidently, he had watched me every morning running for the bus in my high heels – and I was always 10 minutes late by the bus schedule. No one ever carried heels in a bag, wearing sneakers or flats like they do today. I arrived home from the bus stop exhausted.

Ted waited for me one evening and asked me to dinner. I picked the Blue Fox, one of the many five-star restaurants in the City. The waiter seated me and my first thought was of Momma. I wanted her there to enjoy the great things in life – Oh! How I missed her. Her life as a mother of seven was a nightmare every day because of Daddy's meanness when he drank. One day a neighbor curled her hair with pin curls and waves and I remember her being beautiful. She was so pleased! When Daddy saw it that night he put her head in a sink of water. I screamed at him and cried for hours silently.

Ted and I went to his apartment after dinner and had many drinks. Even at 22 years of age, I was very naïve about having a boyfriend. I loved his arms around me. I felt so secure. The evening was wonderful and I was anxious to have a beautiful restaurant breakfast.

As Max and Jennie and I settled into our fabulous furnished apartment on Broadway, we had to move bedrooms every month. Two of us shared and the other got the room to herself. Jennie was pretty strict and rigid. We took turns every week cooking and I hated that because I didn't know how and didn't care. I wanted to try every restaurant in San Francisco. Max didn't date but had beautiful clothes and shoes. She taught me a lot about special foods and drinks. One evening we both wanted to know more about after-dinner drinks, so we walked across the street after dinner and asked the bartender to show us all about them. We had eight or nine different colored drinks in different shaped glasses. We finally decided to walk back across the busy street home. I threw up before I fell asleep.

Our Sunday dinners were like I had as a kid in my first foster home. Lots of food, with a leg of lamb or pork roast, or beef. I didn't cook like that but I set a beautiful table. With or without guests, our conversations would get Jennie so upset. She was very left-brained, with not much humor, so I would always answer a serious question with some off-the-wall remark. When I asked if she had to lose either her eyes or her ears which would she pick? Naturally I would take the opposite one with every reason I could think of, and then just watch her. I knew we were both right. Of course, all three of us were raging liberals, and we talked a lot about Napoleon's saying, "that while the rest of the world sleeps, the high yellow would take over." We weren't scared. It was still the late fifties and early sixties. None of us knew what low yellow was; so why worry about the high yellow.

I had a blind date for dinner with Bob from Portland. I didn't care for him and I told Jennie that he was too serious for me, so she dated him. I never mentioned the blind date to Ted. They decided to marry and she went back to Portland and that broke up our wonderful apartment on Broadway. After two years my social graces were fine-tuned and my cooking improved.

It was still the late fifties. One Saturday night, Ted asked me to move in with him in his beautiful tall apartment building with a view of the Golden Gate Bridge, so I did. Max moved back east and I didn't have much money for a twenty-two-year-old. I had a good job, nice clothes, and like I said, finely honed social skills. I told everyone at work that we were living together and I would get a few gasps from older people. How naïve and sweet I was!

Oh, I forgot to say that at our Sunday dinners it would have been a good time to talk about sex but we never did. I had no one to share my excitement of having oral sex with Ted or taking a shower together. I loved it all, but because we never talked about it, I just figured only prostitutes did that stuff. Oh well! We even had sex two times a day and with my first orgasm, I thought that meant I was pregnant. It was all so hush-hush and stupid.

My life at twenty-four was pretty good. I worked, ate lovely dinners with Ted, for two years, and had no dreams of getting married as Ted did. He did insist that I get my driver's license and the feelings of freedom just overwhelmed me. I was happy just floating through life, living in the now with no goals, dreams, or desires. San Francisco was where I wanted to be.

It was strange that one day Ted's mom called me at work. She told me that Ted had shot himself, and that the bullet missed his heart and that he was alive. I raced to the hospital to see him, along with his former wife and mom. Ted had two small children with her. What I didn't know was that he was having terrible money problems and he was starting to drink during the day and not going to work.

Shit! Was he a copy of my dad? I knew I needed to get away from him. So, I moved out of our apartment and into another fabulous one with great roommates. I never saw Ted again. That was too scary for me.

About once a year I would hear from my sister Lorraine, who was an alcoholic, as was John, her husband. We never really bonded as kids and I had no idea where my brothers were. Lorraine called one evening and said she had a blind date for me and that she and John were bringing him to my apartment on Broadway. I begged her not to and I was really unhappy to open the door and see all three of them. I said hello and then put my hand out and said,

"Hi, I'm Helen."

He replied with "Hi, I'm your brother Larry!"

I almost fainted. It really was a blind date because I hadn't seen him since I was 9 years old, when he visited my foster home in his Marine dress blues. We sat at the kitchen bar and I opened a bottle of wine. I asked many questions about his stay in Bataan and he started to cry. God! What do I do with my older brother? I felt horrible. I was embarrassed that he was crying. I felt shame because we all had the same awful father, and the truth was we didn't talk about it, we didn't trust and we didn't feel. I didn't know how serious it all was. I was too busy honing my great social skills. Four years later in Los Angeles, he was drunk, jumped off the balcony of his apartment, and missed the pool. I have no details because we never talked about it.

With Ted out of my life and a new apartment with wonderful roommates, I was headed for happiness. We had the usual cocktail parties and great dinners, and was even getting fairly good in the kitchen. Mary, one of my roommates, wanted to fix me up for a Thanksgiving dinner date that weekend. I was reluctant, but decided to go. She was engaged to the blind date's partner in a law firm. Without Ted's car, I had to ride down the Peninsula with them. Skip was a tall, blond man who was fixing the whole traditional dinner. He had a cottage near the ocean and it was really quite nice. There were too many drinks. It seemed like a fairly nice evening as I paced myself with all of the booze!

It's a good thing that I didn't drive because I was out of it. I looked around for my roommate and her fiancée, but they were gone. I asked if I could go to sleep and I climbed into Skip's bed. I figured he would bring me back to the city in the morning. I dropped off to a really deep, drunk sleep when I felt Skip climb in next to me. He was interested in having sex and I was too out of it. But that didn't matter, I just wanted to thank him for the nice evening. This was the sixties. We had some sort of drunken sex! All I really remember was when I put my hand between legs, I felt something that was all wet! What the hell was a condom? I had never seen one in my life. Remember Ted had a vasectomy, and even with Ted, and my first orgasm, I thought that I was pregnant! Why didn't any of my roommates ever talk about sex? I was so naïve, and still Pollyanna.

My roommates were having sex. Could I have been the only one who was so naïve? I never talked about sex with anyone ever! Birth control was so far off the charts, and I was so shy. Oh no! Then I remembered Betty, my foster mother, talking to me at fifteen years old, with a long lecture, and I only remembered umbilical cord! I was as uninterested then as I was at twenty-seven. I wanted the easy sex life like I had with Ted.

I was pretty hung over the next day on Friday, but Skip and I took a long walk up the hill which overlooked the Pacific Ocean. I do not remember any dialogue we might have had, or even the long ride back to my apartment in the City. But on Saturday morning, I knew I was pregnant!

My mind just started to whirl in circles. Abortion? No, I will deal with this. Who do I tell? No one! What do I do first? I never thought about a baby. I just thought about being pregnant and not being married! I never thought about Skip once. My fucked-up survival skills were now in high gear and I was scared shitless. What was I scared of? Doing this by myself! I never kept secrets, because I talked too fast and I didn't really have a healthy filter on my mouth or mind.

Well, it's Monday morning and I really don't feel any differently, except that my period didn't start on Saturday like clockwork. I worked for eight engineers and in the office next to me was where Gary worked. He was very smart and we joked a lot in the office and I heard through the grapevine that he wanted to ask me out. When he finally did, I suggested that he come to my place for dinner. I served the identical dinner that I had with Skip, because it was fast and simple. A lot of before wines, dinner wines and dessert wines.

I believe that I was so far out of my body that my ugly survival skills took over my life! Gary got loaded, and before the next week I told him I was pregnant. He seemed to be happy with the thought of a baby coming, and shortly after Christmas, we went to Las Vegas and got married in the Little Chapel of the Chimes. I really don't remember much of that time but one picture brings back a few memories. Both of us quit our jobs after all the office parties and I couldn't wait to get out of the city and start fresh. How does Mill Valley sound? I didn't see Skip again for almost twenty-five years.

On Labor Day, I went into labor of my own and our darling Valerie was born. Not too little at eight pounds twelve ounces, with ten pounds of black hair! But I pulled it off in two hours! We talked about having her born and San Francisco and we wanted her to have the best education. Other than that, welcome to parenthood! After our first year in the small apartment, I found a three-bedroom, two bath house in Mill Valley. I was a stay-at-home mom and I loved doing everything in a perfect way. And I do mean everything! I took care of the house on the inside with all the painting and kept the outside in a pristine manner. I loved working in the garden. I didn't even struggle at being perfect because I had done it all my life. It was my way of not getting into trouble and listening to arguments or being in one myself. I think it's called anal! The house was always cleaned to perfection with fresh flowers and candles everywhere, the grass was mowed and all the decorating was done by me! Gary seemed to approve of everything. If I strived for perfection, there won't be any fighting and no one will yell at me, and I might get praise! We always had wine with dinner and candlelight, and Valerie was fed and bathed by the time Gary arrived home. Painting the whole house for me was a joy. I loved projects and always finished them. Painting sent me into the ozone layer where I could meditate or maybe escape. After all, I did learn to paint in my first foster home.

11
THAT SWEET MAN KILLED HIMSELF

It was a day that couldn't decide to be cloudy or sunny.

Gary and I had been married for four years. Like others we had our hills and valleys. I don't even remember what transpired to keep Gary from not speaking to me for ten days. He never said, "Pass the salt." or "Thank you for the nice dinner." He just got up from the table and went into the den to watch TV. Many times, I would talk to the fridge and hear him laugh at my funny comments when I talked to myself.

On the tenth day, I sat up in bed and said to myself, "I was not put on this earth to take this crap from anyone!" From memories of my mother I refused to take any kind of abuse. Ten days of silence is a long time. I had already been putting up with his nighttime drinking. I was very fortunate that Gary was not a violent person or physically abusive. However, the drinking and the silent treatment led me to divorce. Maybe neither one of us was happy. I had learned not to argue or fight with men because I had one incident with Ted which I said, "For two cents I would smack you in the face for that comment." His reply was a real eye opener to me. His comment was, "If you act like a man I will treat you like a man!" WHOA!

It was Monday morning and I called my lawyer and said, "I know it's your role to try to talk me out of this but I want a divorce…now!" He said OK and dropped the papers off to Gary that night. He told him he needed to be out of the house by the weekend.

I told Valerie that her dad was out of town and he called home constantly during his two months in the apartment that he found in the City. He wanted to come home and I said, "Only if you agree to therapy!" I picked a smart woman with a doctorate, so we could cover all the bases.

The first meeting that we had, the doctor gave us large pieces of butcher paper to draw our family trees. As the baby of seven, I had a tree with branches all over the paper. Gary's drawing, as an only child, was a small picture of three people; his mom, dad, and himself as stick figures. She decided that she would work with him first, and that lasted about a month before he quit seeing her. But he had moved back home.

I never asked him anything and figured he was pretty healthy after seeing her. About 6 months later, when he was supposed to be dressed for breakfast, he came to the dining room in his shorts and t-shirt, and sat on the floor in the corner, with his arms around his knees. He had such a wonderful dry sense of humor, that I joked with him and told him to go get dressed before Valerie got up. Breakfast was ready! He went down the hall to the bedroom and didn't come out. Now I was getting a little upset. I fed Valerie and walked into the bedroom and saw him sitting on the end of the bed in his underwear, just crying. I was so devastated, I didn't know what to do. I hugged him and said, "What's wrong, honey?" He just said, "I don't know!"

I called my neighbor to come and take Valerie for the day. I raced to the phone to call Dr. Lee, our family GP, and he explained that he wasn't trained to help him and gave me a therapist's number. He also suggested that I take him for a drive up to Mt. Tam for lunch where he could calm down. As we sat on the deck overlooking our beautiful county and the Bay, we had a beer. Gary didn't feel like talking and I didn't know what to do or what was wrong.

He only said as we looked out, "It's so peaceful!"

A few days later, Gary decided to take a leave from his job and he was so worried that everyone knew he wasn't okay. I assured him that they didn't know, and he started his therapy sessions again. Some nights he would tell me what was said in therapy or he didn't want to talk about it.

I don't remember what he did all day but about two months into his therapy he told me what was being discussed. He said that when he was 18, about to enter the Naval Academy, he drove his car off a steep ravine, and the police couldn't believe he was the driver as he stood talking to them in his bare feet. Other times he totaled 2 cars. He explained that he was trying to take his own life. He was better now because he was in therapy and he had some pills to keep him from being sad, at least that was the way I saw it.

Later, he began to discuss his therapy sessions and he told me when he was 8 years old when he got up at night to get water, he saw his mom on the sofa with the mailman. His dad traveled often when Gary was little and that was when his alcoholic mother would beat him with a coat hanger if he did something she didn't like. She would then pick up the dog and say, "Rocky, wasn't he a naughty boy?"

I thought of my violent dad and those three stick figures on the drawing.

Spring of 1967 came and another three months passed. Gary ate well, had a couple of glasses of wine in the evening and played the piano. I knew everything was going to be fine, because we had a name for Gary's sadness and he had his pills. In the sixties, it was called Depression. No one talked about it or had it. Just Gary!

After a nice dinner, Gary asked me to fill the gas tank as he forgot to do it. I was so exhausted and fell into bed and slept like a log. When I awoke in the morning, Gary wasn't in bed. He wasn't fixing breakfast, or jogging and what was that God-awful smell? As I went towards the kitchen, it got worse and I opened the kitchen door to the garage and wondered why it smelled so. I walked around the car and saw Gary, dressed in a robe that I had made him, lying in the back seat sleeping. When I opened the car door to shake him awake and saw his grey skin, my body was filled with shame.

I said, "Gary, get out of there before Valerie gets up."

I thought he was asleep as I flung open both garage doors to get out the smell. I thought about the greyness of his skin as I went back in the dining room. Could the paper on the table be his suicide note?

The note on the table said, "I am so tired and so depressed!" I went right into survival mode by calling a neighbor to take Valerie to school. She had been in Montessori school since she was three years old and she needed to be with her friends. I don't know if I was in shock from finding Gary dead in the car but I did call my friend Mary for help.

Mary was at my door when I brought Valerie home from the hospital as a newborn. I was very naïve about a new baby. I always felt their arms and legs would fall off and I had no idea that a baby even needed a bath. Consequently, I had no bathtub for this eight pounder so Mary and I just bathed her in a salad bowl. I was so grateful for all of Mary's help.

When Mary arrived, she was also in shock and kept insisting that he was alive. I knew he was dead. We kept walking from the kitchen to the garage laughing and crying, spilling our tea while checking on him to see if Mary was right and if he was alive. Mary was a want-to-be nurse which made her think she was always right.

Mary wanted me to call Dr. Lee. I put on the tea kettle and decided to call my lawyer. He told us to call the police. It was all over in maybe one hour but we didn't stop checking on Gary during that time. His body was gone and they insisted I pick out a casket by 4:00 that day. Everything was just so fast. The feelings in my body were as cold and dead as Gary.

His note said he wanted to be buried by his grandma in Los Angeles, so after a very large service in Mill Valley, I flew with his body down south for a second service.

I didn't take Valerie to the services, but I did take her to therapy. When I told Valerie he died and wasn't coming back, she, at four, said "We need to take his clothes out of the closet and give them to the poor people!" That was it. Don't talk. Don't trust. Don't feel.

We didn't cry.

That dear, sweet man was gone and I went into a rage. Thinking that it was unfair that he would kill himself and leave me to raise Valerie by myself. What the hell did I know about being a mom? I wanted to explode and oh, how I wanted Momma to come and comfort me.

My dentist told me I needed a crown on my tooth and my neighbor told me my tires on the car were smooth and I knew nothing about either one. I didn't even know how to write a check! And I was 30 years old. But that pushed me over the ledge. I sat down at the dining room table and sobbed for three hours. I then, bought four new tires, got my tooth crowned, and never looked back.

I put everything in storage, rented my house and we moved to Lausanne, Switzerland. We had money in our savings and thank God Gary had left money for Valerie and me. Gary always kept ten thousand dollars in our checking account and I didn't even know how to write a check. We flew to New York and sailed over to the South of France in time for the Cannes Film Festival, on a beautiful Italian Liner.

Valerie had a slight temperature the night before our departure. At my dinner table of eight people there was a Belgian doctor. From the symptoms I gave him he diagnosed it as chicken pox. His responsibility was to tell the captain. Valerie was in quarantine for eight days while I was having an affair with the Italian ships doctor.

Our hotel in Cannes was beautiful and in the evenings, I would go to the bar at 5:00 and have a martini. I became friendly with the bartender while Valerie played and ran around the courtyard with her abacus.

I never saw the man who finally bought me a martini the third night. He found Valerie first and asked her where her father was and when she told him he was dead, that was when he came to my table. We talked and he invited us to lunch the next day. I never thought about our safety. He spoke English and was very kind; that was all I needed. He sent a car to pick us up the next day. We both looked lovely and were excited. Lonely no more.

We kept driving up the mountain to a small town named Grasse, where most of the perfumes are made. The double gates opened onto an exquisite garden and a large white mansion.

There he and his wife stood to greet us with a butler in a tuxedo. I couldn't believe my eyes at the beautiful home, view, and especially the dining table. Valerie asked which fork to use and I told her to start at the outside and work towards the plate. After our martinis, we started to eat. This lovely lunch was served by 2 waiters. I told them we were leaving for Lausanne the next day and sent them flowers and a thank you note. The bartender asked me if I knew who that man really was. When I said that I did not, he explained that he was the President of the World Bank. I almost fainted. Maybe my heart was beginning to mend. I was away from my shitty mother-in-law who blamed me for Gary's death, had no real family, and me being spiritually bankrupt. That lunch was the highlight of my new life and maybe God had decided to come back and show me some wonderful people.

I knew I was running from reality, but I just wanted to rest my heart.

12
TO SWITZERLAND AND HOME

My disconnection from my body had me believing that the Governor of Arkansas, Orval Faubus, was the reason I was in Switzerland. I was bombarded with the segregation problem on TV and his not wanting the black children to go to school with white children made me sick. The National Guard, the dogs, and Gary killing himself, pushed me into doing what I only knew. If I run away, everything will finally get better.

All I remember of the year in Switzerland was that Valerie and I took a Japanese flower arranging class. I remembered some of my high school French, and met a few people who helped me despite the language barrier. The kindest was a Chinese-American doctor, one of the people we ate dinner with every evening, who worked for the United Nations. His family was already living in Lausanne. His twelve-year-old daughter was studying ballet, his eighteen-year-old son was avoiding the draft for the Vietnam War, and his wife, spoke no English. His son met us when we arrived at the train station and took us up to the new apartment that he found for us. I bought a car and followed the taxis around to learn the city. Our apartment was on Lake Geneva and being near the water always soothed my soul, just like San Francisco.

I felt so out of my body living in Switzerland and I wondered if I would do any grieving for Gary. Valerie seemed happy with her dolls and toys. Valerie had a wonderful imagination at four years old. When I asked her what she saw as we laid by the burning fireplace she said, "I see a thousand dancing eyes." There were no more tears but I found the Swiss people very boring and there was only boring butter lettuce for a salad. The neighbor lady even called the police on me for forgetting to put a tie around my garbage bag. I recall that there was always a row of purple daisies and a row of yellow daisies planted in the park and oh, how I wanted to mix them up!

It was very difficult meeting Swiss families or being invited into their homes. I did meet an American named Kristen, whose husband, Sam, was an international lawyer. We would get together for wine and let the kids play. Her son, Timmy, was four and was Valerie's new playmate. Because the lifestyle was not like San Francisco, I needed to get out of there! But first we had to find a nanny.

We climbed into my car and drove to Paris, past acres of yellow flowers blooming for mustard season in Dijon. I drove the last few miles into Paris and into that God-awful traffic around the Arch de Triumph. I immediately fell in love with the city just as I had San Francisco 10 years earlier.

While in Switzerland, Valerie and I did go as far north as Stockholm, and all through Italy but I think I was ready to come home. Fearful despair happened again and again, my roots were in Marin. I was sad. Infinitely sad and scared. I didn't have any plans. I never had long or short-term goals.

Valerie wanted and needed a dog, so we naturally got a black French Poodle and named him after the town where he was born, Boussens! We already had Percy 1, a black cat that we left with the tenant. So now there would be four of us. What was I thinking? – There was no thinking!

A couple of friends met us at the airport with our year's supply of luggage and a dog, and put us up until we could find a place that I could paint. I bought a car, got us an apartment, and put Valerie in school with her former friends.

I was sleeping fitfully and always had a horrible flood of black memories. Being back home, I couldn't go by the house that I owned because of Gary's incomprehensible actions there. However, I tried to get a life going for us. Valerie started piano and I had tennis, I even became the Brownie troop leader. She was doing alright in school, seemed happy, but at 5 years was still wetting her bed! Many of the doctors I saw just told me to leave her alone, that she would quit when she was ready! I found a new peace and happiness in tennis. I played six hours every day for years, with a lesson every Monday. Nothing stopped me or my greatest group of friends from loving tennis. We dried the courts with beach towels, wore scarves, hats, gloves, and long pants when it was cold. We laughed a lot. I was rich in friendships and finally my inner compass was coming back. I felt it was OK to struggle against the tears. "Fine, thank you!" was my new mantra when asked how I was.

13
GYPSY BOOTS TO SPAIN

I wasted two years with a boyfriend named David who was a pathological liar. I was convinced that it was my job to untangle his lies. I finally discovered that when I uncovered one lie there would always be another. He did, however, play great tennis and piano and he taught me to waterski! Why did I waste two years! Goodbye, David!

I talked my friends, Connie and Thora, into going to Carmel for the Clint Eastwood Celebrity tennis tournament. Three days at Pebble Beach was fun, especially talking to Bill Cosby, who really made me laugh until he kept following us all over town. He showed up in all the restaurants where we tried to eat. Sometimes we would leave by the backdoor if we saw him. We were in and out of bars and up and down quaint little alleys until we felt like we lost him. But no, he always appeared where we were. We were waiting for a table when he came up behind me, rubbed his body against my back, put his hand over my right shoulder and grabbed my right breast. I was so shocked and at twenty-one I would have said, "Oh Bill, you are so silly." Instead, at thirty-eight, I yelled, "What the hell do you think you're doing?!"

He just said, "Have a nice dinner ladies."

And was out of there. We never saw him again and were glad he finally left us alone. We watched some tennis the next day and then headed for the drive home. I was still wondering why he grabbed my boob.

Two of my friends had villas in Spain and my gypsy boots are calling me from the closet. I packed again for a year, put everything in storage and moved to Almaneca, just north of Malaga on the Costa del Sol, a small fishing village.

I had started to burn out on tennis. Watergate was just starting and I had a buyer for my Mustang. I was ready!! I had my daughter, a dog from Switzerland and our cat from Mill Valley. My friend, Mimi, met us in Malaga, and we stayed with her for a few days until I found us a gorgeous villa.

I bought a car and we quickly made friends, but I was a city girl and the fishing village wasn't for me. So, I had a girlfriend drive me to the other side of Malaga to show me everything. I settled for Marbella, and while lunching, a friend passed by who knew of a villa for rent right where we were at Puerto Jose Banus. It took me one day to find some broke American college kids to load my car and their car and move all our four of us with a year's supply of luggage about an hour away. I couldn't have been happier as I found a small thatched roof school with all Spanish kids for Valerie to attend. I was ready to explore the neighborhood. Some huge yachts were docked there and owned by very famous, rich people. There were some wonderful restaurants and great dress shops. I had found my community!

People were so friendly to Americans and I was introduced to Harold, an older guy from New York who was interested in theatre. Enough so that he wanted to start some form of a country club and theatre because Americans were sticking together too much. I loved organizing our thoughts and ideas and we pulled together a theatre group and we called it ITS, or International Theatre Studio. There was so much talent there and anyone who spoke English was welcomed. We tried to do two plays a year and we had 500 members. I loved being a producer and once an understudy for a Neil Simon play. I had no desire to be an actor and just loved projects. These plays took lots of work but they were very professional. Some of the people living there had experience in RADA (the Royal Academy of Dramatic Arts).

All of the members looked forward to a big New York opening. Lights, pictures taken for the newspaper, getting really dressed and going to dinner, and meeting the cast.

I loved what I was doing and Valerie was happy with her friends and her Spanish was fluent. So, I called the storage place back home and told them to not sell my stuff. I thought I would stay a second year.

Valerie and I had our first serious talk when she was eleven as we walked up the small hill to the riding stables in Spain.

She asked me, "Mom, how did daddy die?"

My knees almost buckled and I said, "I don't think we'll ride today as we need to go home so I can tell you the whole story."

My therapist had told me not to explain too much to a four-year-old and just wait until she asked. Today was that day.

We both loved our life in Marbella, Spain and our villa was just what we needed. Marble floors for the dog and the cat to chase each other happily. It was good. I knew I would do my best explaining Gary's death to her but I knew that I knew nothing about Depression. Being an Aries, I don't get sick, don't like sick, don't want to talk about sick and would make a lousy nurse or doctor. I thought if I could just stay calm and make everything perfect Gary would have snapped out of those moods with the help of a doctor and some medication. Holy shit! I was thirty going on seventeen!

I tried to talk about chemical imbalance, change of moods, but I didn't know what I was talking about. She seemed satisfied with my explanation and that was it. We hugged but never talked about it again.

Most of the same people worked hard to start a country club for English speaking people from all over Europe. We used a large hotel called El Paraiso for their kitchen and ball room for all of our activities. So we called it EPIC (El Paraiso International Club). It was like home a lot, with tennis and golf tournaments, swimming and every themed party you could think of. We had 600 happy members. Again, I called the storage place back home and said to push my stuff to the back, as I was staying one more year. Valerie was now in a British school and I was a room mom helping with lunches and everything else that we needed.

For the third year, Valerie went to a boarding school in Malaga, as our landlord taught there and he took her and brought her home on Friday evenings. We were happy but we missed each other. I could work on the activities of the theatre and the club. Again, life was good. It was a case of having Yankee ingenuity while there, find a need and fill it. We worked hard to get American movies in the theatre and the manager got us popcorn. He couldn't understand popcorn for us, and we couldn't understand sunflower seeds for them. But everyone was happy.

At the end of the third year, I decided that there would be no more private schools or boarding schools. Franco had just died and Spain was getting King Juan Carlos. It was time to hit the American Public High School and without really knowing the area, except that it was close to Grandma Dee and Grandpa Gus (Gary's parents) I landed in Corona del Mar. I just had to be by the water and it was in Orange County. I put Valerie in the high school and I got a job with a consulting firm and we operated one of the big yacht clubs. I could never feel a sense of community there like

Marbella, Spain or Marin County. After one year, my neighbor told me I was not in culture shock, that this was the heart of the Republican Party and the right-wing Christian coalition. That answered all my questions and it took me only two months to get the moving van and get out of there. We were headed back home to Marin; Valerie and the dog and cat and me. Back home where we started.

Things had drastically changed when I got back home.

I was now away five years and when I stopped in my post office, the postman said, "Hi, Helen! How was Spain?"

I knew what home and community were! Valerie was doing her last two years in high school with friends from second and third grades, and girls she had been in the Brownie troop with.

My friend Thora's husband, Bob, was having an affair with her best friend, and she was drinking and heading for divorce court. Connie was drinking too much and physically fighting with her husband. It was all a mess. Tennis was our only outlet, and I was starting a new chapter again. It was going to be okay.

Now all of our kids were ready to graduate from high school. Valerie was off to Paris at 17 by herself to attend the Sorbonne.

We made it through those last teen years and we were both ready for a change. Boy was she brave, she would be eighteen in one month.

What next is gonna' land on my plate?

14
FORMICA AND NAUGAHYDE

It was a sunny morning in 1986 when I stopped at the bank. I needed breakfast and across the street was Denny's, a place I had never been with all my years in Marin. The place was empty and I couldn't take a booth in case a large family came. This, I learned, was part of my hypervigilance I had from childhood and was working on with my therapist. She also told me that I had PTSD. What was that? I have never had a headache in my life.

There was one elderly woman at the counter alone so I sat myself next to her. She was very elegant in her silk dress, three strands of pearls and many beautiful rings.

"That looks good," I said, "What did you order?"

Her beautiful smile relaxed me. We did small talk and then she started telling me about her nephew.

She lived in an exclusive part of San Francisco called Pacific Heights. I had lived there also in my single days with roommates. She moved here from Washington D.C. because her sister was very sick and about to die. She kept telling me how lonely she was except for the time she saw her nephew. They seemed to be very close. We laughed, shared stories, and decided to meet there the next Saturday.

She invited me to her home many times and I helped her

change lightbulbs that were too high or mop the floor where she couldn't reach. I was learning more about her nephew and thought he might be a person I had known. She told me how she didn't like his wife and how much she wished that I could marry him. He was a lawyer in the city and I felt the tears start to roll down my cheeks as she spoke. Was it intuition? How did I know?

Twenty-five years had gone by and I had not seen him. But I knew...Her nephew was the father of my daughter. Holy shit! She didn't see me cry but I left and cried all the way home across the Golden Gate Bridge.

We made a promise to meet every Saturday for brunch and we did. My secret was still mine. We drove to Napa one sunny day to plant Ivy on her sister Evelyn's plot at the cemetery. This would have been my mother-in-law if all those years ago I hadn't gone into shame and made my big secret. I was so young and naive and my survival skills were all screwed up. I dug the hole and she put in the ivy. We must have had thirty or forty ivy pots and as I pushed the shovel into the solid earth, I wondered what God had in store for me.

15
OVER THE INVISIBLE LINE

What the hell was going on? My friends were falling apart right in front of my eyes – Barb had lung cancer from all the smoking and drinking, Connie had a stroke from not stopping both and Thora who never smoked got two DUI's before 10:00 A.M. on the same day! Connie developed diabetes and lost one leg, and when I visited her I would walk in singing and she would immediately start harmonizing, just as before her stroke. Her hair was white now, she was in a convalescent hospital, and had divorced her abusive husband years earlier. The three of us were so sick and yet we were like sisters. Thora was financially responsible for Connie, so her last days were made very comfortable with her huge savings.

Because of her DUI's, Thora headed off to rehab for 90 days, instead of going to jail, which doesn't help. I was burning out on tennis, and I couldn't believe Thora was an alcoholic in rehab. I drove 30 minutes into the wine country to visit her on the weekend. I never put the two together. Alcoholic rehab and the Napa Valley wine country in the same place? I attended AA meetings with her and hung out by the pool.

I studied the literature carefully but wasn't sure if my father fit into anything that I read. Even my oldest sister, Jeanne, didn't look like an alcoholic because she didn't get angry or swear, or bounce off walls and she always wore a hat! How could she be? My idea of an alcoholic was always old men asleep in the doorways, or living on the street.

When I told Thora that she didn't look like an alcoholic, she became upset and told me never to say that again. Because if she didn't look it, she could fool people and take a drink! Boy, did I have a lot to learn.

When her 90 days were over, I attended a chip meeting with her. She drove and I had a fit because I thought we were lost. She tried to convince me that we had the right place. But it looked like a kids' basketball gym with all the young boys acting happy! When she told me they were alcoholics and getting their chip for time in the program, I kept thinking of my dad and my sister. Could they be? No, not her, but he could be! And those young boys, how could they be alcoholics?

I took all the literature I could get and then a nice lady said that maybe I would like to learn more from Al-Anon. Alcoholism is a family disease. I have 5 brothers and sisters – could they be? What about me? Am I?

My feelings were all over the map, I was crying a lot for the next week and laughing a lot also. I wanted to run away from myself but I kept seeing my dad's face as well as my oldest sister, Jeanne. Was I headed towards Pandora's Box? I knew I had so much stuff buried, but I had no way of knowing how to retrieve it and did I want to? I was really scared and crying a lot. I had no one to talk to about these feelings and what if I was wrong? Why was I crying so much and still saying, "Fine, thank you!"

I called and got the Al-Anon schedule but waited about a week to attend. I knew I didn't want to go where there were men because like that AA meeting I attended, they all had my dad's face. It just was too scary. So off I went Wednesday night to a room full of women. I felt safe and I knew I was home from all the stories I heard. Women were crying as they shared their stories. Some had dads who drank and some had moms and husbands. I wasn't the only one any more as I always thought. That was my great secret. These women were letting go of that awful secret and I was going to also. I attended a meeting every night and couldn't get enough information and still wasn't sure if my dad and sister were alcoholics. One book said that the alcoholic usually kills the family pet and my dad took our dog, Bob, away and had him put to sleep. Reading that was the horrific jolt that I needed. I stood up in my meeting and shared out loud to everyone that my dad was alcoholic. Now what was I going to do with this information? Was that the end of it? My tears? All of those unresolved feelings and was my sister also? Could women & children be alcoholics? I was both happy and sad to learn all of this. I wasn't scared anymore because I was so safe in those meetings and I was making friends with so many wonderful people! I shared something every meeting and it was mostly about my daughter who was so angry with me that I hadn't seen her for almost a year. She had her own job and apartment and I would hear from one of her friends occasionally that she was just fine. I don't know why she was angry because we didn't communicate at all. My heart was so broken! And the things I was learning about alcoholism were just so overwhelming. I had not only my sister, Jeanne as an alcoholic, but a brother and my sister who was 15 months older than me. They were all admitted alcoholics. Shit! What do I do with this information? And where was my daughter? I now called myself an ACA or Adult Child of an Alcoholic. I am about to learn what effect this all had on my relationships, my employment, my finances and my daughter.

My first awakening came when one woman, living with her boyfriend, was consistently beaten. At each meeting, she would say that "he only broke my finger, not my arm" and the room was silent. Months later, she said again, "I am getting tired of being his doormat! I kicked him out because I'll be damned if I'm gonna be wall-to-wall carpet!" The room of 200 women screamed, applauded, cried, hugged and left with more Hope! Especially me!

My thoughts turned to abusive behavior. My poor Momma was beaten almost on a daily basis –
My husband gave me the silent treatment for ten days and I filed for divorce.
My daughter always hung up on me. She used phrases like "you've hurt my feelings" and "I'm so sensitive!" and I told her to get the book called "Are you addicted to sensitivity?" Naturally, she hung up!
They say there are two sides to a coin, and by turning it over in your mind you may see the truth. Abuse was as simple as holding your pee too long, driving your car on empty, depriving yourself of sleep.

I thought I would get better faster if I took the training to help women that were abused. The information that I learned completely sucked the energy from my body. Our last class had a male speaker who would tell us, "Why Men Hit Women!" Was God in my life again helping me? Moving me to the next level of healthiness? More facts meant more knowledge to peel the onion. I thanked God and called it G.I.A... God in Action.

I fell apart crying and took a leave from the class. I could feel the denial breaking up in my body. I was retching and I knew about my Dad. I started therapy immediately, and was learning about living in the abyss for years, not knowing how to get to any solutions. All I knew was "Fine. Thank you!" My tool box was getting fuller. I learned that as an ACA, I will agree with everyone and everything. Then I will crawl away and try to put the pieces together. And even if it kills me. I will do it again and again.

I just kept that cycle going for years, because I didn't get it!

I was learning too much too fast from those wonderful women at my meetings.

I will never forget when I heard that... "Forgiveness is not forgetting – it's about letting go of someone's throat!" And "Tears are sometimes the best words the heart can speak!" And I had a boatload full!

16
KICKING THE CRAP OUT OF THE
ELEPHANT IN THE LIVING ROOM

"The need for change bulldozed the center of my mind."
Maya Angelou

"And you cannot go on indefinitely being just an ordinary, decent
good egg. We must be hatched or go bad."
C.S. Lewis

My first meeting was so scary. The lights went out and
they lit a candle as she introduced a different woman to be
the main speaker. Naturally, I sat by the door to make my
fast getaway if something scary was to happen. As she began
to speak, I noticed her soft features, her blond hair and
beautiful smile. She told her family history and how the
twelve steps had worked in her life. Her father was alcoholic
and her mother was always trying to get him to stop. She
talked of how often they fought, and how she herself had
now stopped drinking and doing drugs. She told us that she
had met a nice man in the program and was about to get
married. Now what the hell was that all about? I was not
there to meet any men. I was only there to stop crying. Can
I do all of that by learning three steps a week? Yes, and I

will be out of here in two months. This was stupid. I never knew any female who did drugs, nor was an alcoholic except my friend Thora, and I didn't really believe her. Both of my sisters drank a lot, but I don't think they were alcoholics. How could they be alcoholics? Only men were alcoholics. Maybe I wouldn't go anymore because I was getting too confused.

When the speaker used words like Adult Children of Alcoholics, I heard myself taking these small gasping breaths. Dysfunctional, emotionally unavailable, rigidity, no boundaries and secrets. I was totally flabbergasted and I felt the tears flow down my cheeks. I wanted to yell out "BINGO" because I now knew what she was talking about. Very softly I said, "You're Home, Helen." I knew immediately that whether I liked it or not, there was more I needed to hear. At that meeting a woman asked me if I had anything to share. I started sobbing hysterically saying, "My father drank, was a violent Irishman who shot my mother and then himself when I was eight. "When I stopped, all she said was keep coming back because it worked. Now that really pissed me off. At the same time, it felt good to get so many hugs from strangers, but I still didn't quite know what I was supposed to do. I wanted to feel better and stop crying, but nobody gave me the real secret to happiness. No one made my bad feelings go away. In actuality, I felt worse about the shame of sharing my secret.

As I drove away from the church, I couldn't stop crying. I knew something was happening, but what? I felt so ashamed for spilling my guts and no one even took the time to fix me. It was only 9:30 P.M. and I would have stayed there until midnight to hear any magic words. My body was exhausted and I felt drained when I got home. I knew that I had heard some powerful stuff, but the only couple of things I really remember was that I was an Adult Child of an Alcoholic. That phrase seemed to lift a great deal of weight off of me, but I was still confused. The other phrase was Keep Coming Back, It Works. If everyone there knew I was an Adult Child of an Alcoholic and the room was filled with all those women who were also ACA's, then there must be lots more I needed to learn. If this is why I was sad, then my brothers and sister were also ACA's. My deceased husband, Gary, who only drank in the evenings from 7:00 P.M. to 11:00 P.M., never missed a day of work, must be one. I later learned that he was called a maintenance alcoholic. Now I remember back to my mother-in-law who was always drinking. I also learned that ACA's usually become alcoholics or they grow up and marry one. Well, I certainly did that. I felt like I was split right down the middle because I hated to admit that I belonged in that room with all those women, yet I wanted to be there. I put the box of tissues on the floor, grabbed the cat, Percy 4, shut off the light and fell asleep. I knew I was opening Pandora's Box, and boy was I tired.

I made the friends that I needed to have in my life. Some were in such pain and some were heading up the mountain. Being down in that valley didn't do me or anyone any good. I was building a support group which took away the loneliness. I was learning so much about alcoholism that my head was spinning.

The lady who ran the meeting asked me to help her one evening, as she had a bad back. I literally froze because I was very new and inexperienced. We were scheduled to have a speaker who didn't show, and I was told to just pick a word and let the women talk about it or whatever they needed. That didn't seem so difficult, and in most meetings the word "arrogance" was used often, so I chose its opposite, "humility". The first lady I chose to share said, "I heard you share at all of the meetings we attend and I would like to hear your story." Talk about humility. So this was my first speaking experience in these rooms. The lights went out, the candles were lit, and I began.

There was applause, which I think was not allowed, along with tears and laughter. I thought I would explode with the happiness I felt. Women asked me to sponsor them, wanted to have a coffee with me, and some just wanted a hug. I just loved them all and could feel the love from them. One woman said she felt like she'd been kicked in the stomach! I was not a bowler but I had just cut those bowling balls from my ankles that I had carried all those years. I told all the damn family secrets and they were out there. I was now dealing with my shame.

That experience opened all doors for me. I was asked to speak in San Francisco, Sonoma and home in Marin. Even therapists who heard me recommended that their clients attend this meeting. When the leader's time was over, I was elected to take her place for six months. There was so much to learn about how my dad's drinking affected me; my relationships, money, food, and smoking. I was very willing to do those seven meetings a week. This group of thirty women started in the basement of a church and ended with up to two hundred crying, laughing, and hugging women. I wanted to kill the old pattern of don't talk, don't trust and don't feel. We all knew that we were just beginning to peel the onion and find our authentic selves. There was no more "Fine, Thank you!" Did anyone ever say there was fun in dysfunctional? I knew it should be called DysFUCKtional!

But where was my daughter? She took her hidden anger and was gone on and off for the next twelve years. Only now and then would I hear from her. The birthday cards did not have return addresses. There was not much I could do. My pain was so strong that I went to bed for the first three months and cried, smoked and wrote in my journal, trying to get to some solution. My friends told me that I was addicted to her. That I was going through withdrawals and I was left with an emotional plate of spaghetti to untangle. I felt so alone and couldn't discuss my feelings. I believe that in some small place in my heart, I was desperately hearing the truth call to me, and that her leaving was a great gift, but I didn't need any professional help, because only crazy people needed therapy, and I wasn't there yet. But that didn't stop my heart from being broken. We still had secrets that couldn't be healed without dialogue.

The first thing on my problem-solving list was to come clean with a few secrets that I had buried under my toe nails. The one that brought the most tears was the truth about who was really the father of my daughter. I always knew. I just chose to never talk about it. I thought that it would never need to be known and that I could take this information to my grave if I could only make it all perfect. Don't talk. Don't trust. Don't feel. But right now, I had bigger fish to fry.

17
MY LAST SECRET

Lucille and I continued our lunches. She took me to her women's club in San Francisco. Rather than just drop her off this time, she asked me to come up for a glass of sherry. When she opened the door to this magnificent apartment she said, "Are you here?"

A man answered.

"I'm in the back!"

My gut was on fire. It couldn't be him. She always wanted me to meet her nephew, so this was her sweet way of doing it. Holy shit! Twenty something years later. He walked into the room and I froze. His arms pulled me into a bear hug and he said,

"You haven't changed. You're still as pretty."

And I mumbled something similar. I was so filled with shame and fear I could hardly speak.

Did she know something? No! I never told her anything and he knew nothing. I figured she just told him about our lunches and planting ivy on his mother's plot. I sat and smiled. I don't remember a thing, I might as well have been asleep. Just my way of leaving my body.

When Lucille left the room, I asked Skip if we could meet for a drink some night and just catch up. His place was on top of Nob Hill. I parked and took the elevator to his living room. Something I had never done before. What a view. He made us a drink. His wife was not there and I was prepared, as my toolbox was getting fuller. No Fear. The Truth as I knew it and less shame. Last Secret.

"Cheers!" we said over our wine.

"Do you remember the night twenty-some years ago that you fixed Thanksgiving dinner and I spent the night and we had sex?"

"Of course!" he said, "But Helen, it was two nights."

"Oh my God! We drank too much because I got pregnant and we had a daughter."

He took my hand and said, "Why didn't you tell me? I have never had a child of my own! I would love to have been involved in her upbringing."

He clenched my hands tighter as we sat in silence.

"I don't know." I finally responded. "I went right into Fear and my screwed-up survival skills went into motion. I am so sorry."

I cried and kept saying how sorry I was. We hugged.

"I would never have told anyone about us as this was my secret, but it slipped out one day last year in an argument with Valerie and I denied it. Then Lucille and I met and the wounds were reopened. My husband, Gary, thought she was his daughter and he never knew. He died when she was four. I'm not ready to tell Valerie yet and I don't know why." I cried.

"Well when you are ready I will be with you one hundred percent." He said.

Because Lucille had told me he was unhappy in his marriage, I just guessed that our secret would continue. I hoped I was right.

We hugged again and he took me to my car.

Driving across the Golden Gate Bridge, I still didn't feel well as this wound was wide open and I had some decisions to make. I decided to quit my job and move back to Portland. By cutting off all emotions and getting on with my life, I would find another job and a cute apartment that needed painting.

I packed my belongings and my cat Percy 4, and we drove to Portland to, maybe, spend some time with my old foster mom Betty. She was alone since Gene had passed away. Too many people had passed on including my sister Jeanne, my friend Lucille and my foster dad Gene.

Betty was now in her mid- seventies and never stopped being verbally abusive to me. When I surprised her after getting settled in with friends, she answered the door by saying,

"Portland is mine and San Francisco is yours."

I just thought we could have lunch together since she was now alone. When I was a teen she always called me Pollyanna the Glad Girl. I could always see the best in any situation and she didn't like that.

I told her during one of her abusive times, "If my father couldn't break my spirit why do you think you can?!"

I had a good spiritual church in Portland that believed in the seven major religions. With all my therapy work only I knew I had one bigger secret to reveal. My daughter, when we were in contact, was very verbally abusive to me, because I wouldn't tell her who her father was. I wasn't ready to tell her about her real father. Gary was my husband and Skip was her biological father, but I couldn't tell her when she was so mean. One time her eyes were very foggy like she had a filter over them. She told me she wasn't feeling well and was on some medication and I believed her. When I looked into her eyes, she wasn't there.

I contacted a Los Angeles lawyer and found out that I didn't ever have to tell her.

During one of her abusive episodes I cried, "Why don't you just leave me alone and call me next year when you're twenty-five! I will take you over to San Francisco and introduce you to your real father!" Her silence was deafening and the look on her face put the knife deeper into my heart. She turned around and walked back into her work.

I almost fainted and turned around to see who had said that. Not me because that was buried so deep that no one would ever know. I was dumbfounded that it came out of my mouth. I drove home and didn't allow myself to feel.

It was very scary to tell my whole story to my minister. I was so ashamed and who would like me if I told the truth? My secret was supposed to be safe with me but someone else said, "It's your turn Helen! Step up and do your work!" My minister, Mary, helped me write my daughter and her father, Skip. I wasn't strong enough to do a phone call even though he knew and I had his support when I was ready. If I tried, I wouldn't be able to explain. But as I crossed over the border from California to Oregon, I felt like the umbilical cord was cut. I thought of my first sex talk at fifteen from Betty and only remembering umbilical cord. My daughter was now twenty-five and I sat down and wrote the identical thing to both of them on the same identical card. Which was Picasso's Dove of Peace. I lived in shame. Which one would hate me the most and would they like each other? I said a short prayer as I dropped both cards into the mailbox that rainy day in Portland.

I did not want to be involved in this triangle and when Valerie reached out to Skip they decided to meet for lunch. Which they did on three or four occasions. Valerie did not discuss any of it with me. My secret became hers. Skip and maybe his wife, owned the secret too. I did not see or speak to Skip again. I learned from my therapist that triangles just don't work.

18
ABOUT VALERIE

Valerie's teacher asked me to come to school to talk about Valerie and her behavior. It seems she had taken a pencil and scribbled very hard on the wall. She was seven years old. When I asked three or four doctors why she was still wetting the bed I was told, "She'll quit when she's ready." Or "Leave her alone and don't discuss it." How come I didn't like or believe what the doctor said? Did I believe that blip in my stomach was telling me something?

For dinner in one of our local diners, I told Valerie she could have Jell-O for dessert. The waitress brought the Jell-O with a dollop of whipped cream. I looked in amazement when she told the waitress that she didn't like whipped cream because it "tasted like gray." I had never heard a child say something that descriptive. Could food really taste like gray?

She had horseback riding, piano and playdates, but mostly, she liked being by herself.

Valerie came home from school one day holding a hand delivered invitation from Lucy up on the hill, who was well-liked. She was having a spaghetti and swim party and all the kids were going. She grabbed the mail from the mailbox as I carried the groceries. She was excited to see another invite from Allison, who didn't have many friends. Both birthday parties were on the same day.

I explained that it was her decision to make as to which party she wanted to attend.

Without hesitation, she didn't choose Lucy because she said, "I know all the kids will go to Lucy's and none will go to Allison's."

She was right. Only two kids were at Allison's party.

Many years later I ran into Allison's mother and she thanked me for letting Valerie's go to Allison's party. I felt so wonderful to say that she had made her own right decision.

She was eight when we were in Spain for three years and I started her in a thatched roof school and every evening we both worked on those twenty-four thousand verbs and conjugating them. She was fluent in no time. I still live and speak in the present tense. She loved riding horses there and did well in school. At twelve I decided there would be no more private schools or boarding schools and we headed back to California for the American Public High school. She seemed to be angry about so many things such as making her bed or hanging her clothes. She did not want to help around the house. I picked Corona Del Mar in Southern California so we could be close to Grandma, Grandpa, Aunt Mimi and Uncle Petie. What I didn't know was Valerie and I *both* had secrets.

I wasn't happy in Southern California so I hired a van and we headed back to Marin. There she could hook up with her friends from the old neighborhood and grammar school. Life seemed good. She had a part time job as a waitress, her grades were good, and she was sleeping more but was still anxious. Her whole body seemed to slow down and all she wanted to do was sleep. Our general practitioner had died when Valerie was young so I wasn't sure who to talk to about all of this. Usually I just compared stories of other mothers, teenage back talk and sleeping seemed pretty normal. She did graduate and she was now packing for her trip. She was almost eighteen when I put her on a plane and she moved to Paris, France to live by herself and attend The Sorbonne for one year. Such bravery!

I was exhausted with the arguing, the back talk, but I cried as I watched the plane lift off. This was the beginning of our long and short separations. In later years, I didn't know what state she was in. I cried wondering how she was doing and I smiled at many of the good memories I had of her.

When she was almost twenty-five she called and told me not to be upset and told me that Uncle Petie had molested her when she was six on a weekend visit to Grandmas. He said he would hurt both of us if she told anyone. I was enraged and ready to fly to L.A. to kill him. However, at age eighty-two, he apologized to her and said he only did it because she was so pretty. She forgave him. I still wanted to murder him. All of her headaches, bed wetting until fifteen years old, depression and anxiety were filling in the puzzle for me.

I don't understand depression and the mixed-up medications she must have taken, her necessity to do everything by herself, never asking for help- it was all part of the problem.

I so loved Valerie and hated the phone call from my granddaughter Atessa telling me,

"Mom hung herself with the dog leash in the bathroom."

My heart was broken. If I had only known about what happened when she was six years old. I'm not going around the barn again trying to find out why Valerie killed herself like I had with Gary. I believe she tried to detox herself from anti-depressants and everything just went black.

I still think of her every day.

Oh god I miss her laughter.

I miss singing together and harmonizing to "Dream a Little Dream of Me."

It reminded me of when Momma and I sang.

HELEN HAYES

FINAL THOUGHTS

It has been a year and a half since Valerie's death. Both of my granddaughters are getting stronger and the three of us have come to understand that, as I was told, "grieving is just love with no place to go."

Silence took my childhood, my husband and my daughter. Shame turned my experiences to secrets and silence is not a part of me anymore. I Trust. I Talk. I Feel.

I finally opened the cardboard box I carried from foster home to foster home, sending its contents to my granddaughters so they could have a piece of my heart. A locket, the book titled The Little Engine That Could and a few pictures I had drawn- I don't know what happened to the little blue dress with the strawberries.

I was told when I was having trouble praying to a God that this is what I could say, "God, my heart is open, come sit in my heart."

Today is 2018 and as I think of the good and the awful in my life and why I am the way I am, I must say I believe it started with my birthday- March 29th. I'm an Aries. Mom told me that out of seven kids I was the only one who walked out of the womb. What did that mean? Secondly, coming from a violent family and being the baby of seven I always said yes to everything for fear of being spanked. I believe I am visual because my mama told me to smell the sweet peas and notice the colors. I believe my survival skills were put in to order fast while very young making me resilient.

Here is what I learned:
1. Get to the solution immediately. You either let go or you get dragged.
2. Stay in the present- I put yesterday in a file drawer in my mind called "stuff." I can't delete it but it doesn't rule my heart.
3. Accept whatever is. That's why I love the serenity prayer. However, when it comes to "God grant me..." I changed my prayer to say "God *grants* me..." I didn't want to feel like I was always begging. The serenity was finally mine to take and I did. What a difference that "**S**" makes. Now I constantly say "*Holy Ess!*"

Let me say that getting healthy took eight years of seven meetings a week in the Al-Anon program of Adult Children of Alcoholics. Sometimes we called it Adult Children of Addicts and even Adult Children of Assholes. Well, the day was gonna' go by anyway so it didn't matter, I just showed up.

I had learned to recognize my pain. I tried so hard to fight it with anger and denial. I remember denial meaning, "**D**idn't **E**ven **N**otice **I A**lways Lied." I hid my grief under anger my whole life. Why should I believe in, or turn to God or a Universal being for help, guidance, patience, or love? I was angry at God for taking my brother, my parents, my husband and my daughter.

Shame was a big issue for me. So was being perfect. One loves the other.

In my women's recovery group, I learned about being strong and bouncing back from adversity that can come at any time. Because I lost my brother at seven and my parents at eight I was taught to imagine I was climbing up the high dive at the pool. Slowly climbing up the steps of the ladder and walking to the end of the highest board I could stand there as long as I liked, with no turning back. But at some point, I would have to jump once I believed that there was water in the pool.

I finally trusted that there was something bigger in my life to guide me and I am not afraid to call on that Greater or Universal Power all day long. I am no longer living in my zip code, but rather, the Universe.

I never once said that it was easy but friends say I fit into my own skin now and my former minister always said, "Go to the edge of the light you see!" During our breakup so many moons ago, my ex-boyfriend Ted said to me, "Helen, you need to march to your own drummer." When did I not?

My friend Thora who got me into Al-Anon doesn't play tennis anymore due to a bad back but has spent many years learning the Tango. I tease her about always dancing backwards. Will she ever dance forwards? She has thirty-two years in A.A.

Last Summer I visited my only living brother Don who now has dementia, but did publish a book at eighty-three about his love of the B-17 airplane and his World War II experiences. We talked about being the last two in our family alive and how alcohol killed the other five and how guns killed our parents and brother. He never drank or smoked. He is now ninety-three and with little eyesight, I still write to him and his wife Irene, who is also ninety-three. She is taking very good care of him. Every day she reads him my letters.

My two granddaughters, Atessa and Savannah and I are building a relationship after many years apart during their younger years. Atessa is in Austin, Texas and will be attending veterinary school and Savannah is in North Carolina where she is working on her Master's Degree. Valerie would be so proud, as am I. I want them to be whatever they choose, especially Happy, Joyous and Free!

After Valerie's death we all grieved in our own way, sometimes together on the phone, sometimes with grieving groups and sometimes with private therapists. We will stay strong.

I do believe there is no light at the end of the tunnel. We are the light in the middle of the tunnel. We can never give up. I want to be the voice for the people who are still silent. If my story helps one person I will be grateful.

No more secrets, no more shame, and no more silence. I have my music, my tennis, my volunteer work at the homeless dining room and Mom's Demand Action working to keep guns out of schools, attending Al-Anon meetings at San Quentin Prison and sharing my stories of recovery, my 49er games and my black cat Percy 5.

Well that's about it…As I look around my office where there has been lots of laughter and tears, I think it's time for a fresh coat of paint. So, I'm off again to the paint store. I'll talk to you soon!

Take care of yourselves and each other,
Helen

ABOUT THE AUTHOR

Helen's alcoholic father killed her mother and then himself when Helen was eight years old at her brother's twelfth birthday party. She struggled to break the pattern of her father's legacy, but only years after her husband's suicide and learning of her daughter's death does she ultimately triumph.

Helen resides in Marin County, California.

"Sweet peas in the jelly jar"
I picked those with my mother before her death.

First visit to a beauty salon.

community and the housing people, and strafing the Japanese on the
(Continued on page five.) rocky Aleutian Island.

Tragedy Struck Their Home

Clinging together today, still not fully aware of the full import
of the tragedy which struck their home Saturday evening, were
Helen (left), 8, and Lorraine Hayes, 9. Their father, George
Hayes, 54, shot and killed their mother, Mabel, 41, at Mrs.
Hayes' home, W.1616 College, and then killed himself. The
shooting occurred while the children were celebrating the 12th
birthday of their brother Stanley. Lorraine ran into the house
and tried to drag her mother away. Her father fired a shot in
the child's direction, but it did not hit her, the girl said today.
(News account and other pictures on page three.)

Graduation from grammar and high school

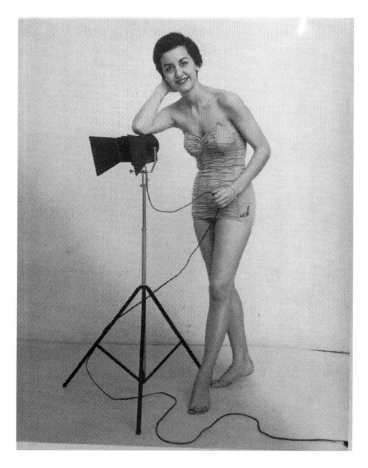

My first modeling job at 17 for Jantzen

Age 22, San Francisco

Second row, second seat from left.

April 26, 2018

Cosby Verdict:

Guilty

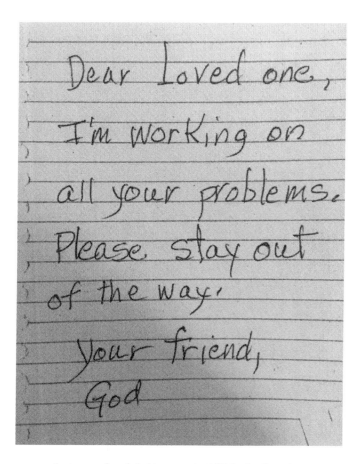

A stranger handed this to me in 1986 after I spoke.

Made in the USA
Columbia, SC
29 October 2024